Have You Ever Been Bitten by an Elephant?

THE DEFINITIVE GUIDE FOR RETIRING WELL

David S. Blackston
with Drew Blackston

Blackston Financial Advisory Group
THE VILLAGES, FLORIDA

David Blackston/Blackston Financial Advisory Group
8564 East CR 466, Suite 302
The Villages, FL 32162
www.blackstonfinancialgroup.com

Book layout ©2013 BookDesignTemplates.com

Ordering Information:
Quantity sales. For details, contact the address above.

Have You Ever Been Bitten by an Elephant?/ David Blackston. —1st ed.
ISBN 978-1530600236

or the rendering of personalized investment advice for compensation, over the Internet. Any subsequent, direct communication by Blackston Financial Advisory Group with a prospective client shall be conducted by a representative that is either registered or qualifies for an exemption or exclusion from registration in the state where the prospective client resides. For information pertaining to the registration status of Blackston Financial Advisory Group, please contact the state securities regulators for those states in which Blackston Financial Advisory Group maintains a registration filing. A copy of Blackston Financial Advisory Group's current written disclosure statement discussing Blackston Financial Advisory Group's business operations, services, and fees is available at the SEC's investment adviser public information website – www.adviserinfo.sec.gov or from Blackston Financial Advisory Group upon written request. Blackston Financial Advisory Group does not make any representations or warranties as to the accuracy, timeliness, suitability, completeness, or relevance of any information prepared by any unaffiliated third party, whether linked to Blackston Financial Advisory Group's web site or incorporated herein, and takes no responsibility therefor. All such information is provided solely for convenience purposes only and all users thereof should be guided accordingly.

Contents

Foreword by Drew Blackston 1

Preface 5

The Emotions of Dealing With Money 9

Getting the "Big Picture" Through Holistic Planning 17

    The Accumulation Phase 23

    The Preservation and Distribution Phase 24

Passing the Financial Torch 27

A Guaranteed Income or a Maybe Income - Which Do You Want
When You Retire? 39

Fees - The Devil Is in the Details 51

Long-Term Care - The Elephant in the Living Room 57

    The Cost of Long-Term Care 58

Having a Purpose for Your Money 69

Suitability vs. Fiduciary Advice 81

Constructing Your Financial House 95

Treat Your Health Like Your Wealth 103

What's the Deal With Annuities? 113

Getting a Round Tuit 123

Dedicated to the memory of my mother and father, Clifford and Martha Sue Blackston, both deceased. Their struggles caused me to want to make sure none of my clients ever go through what my Mom did when my Dad passed away. I also want to dedicate this book to my mother-in-law and father-in-law, Bill and Martha Jane Evans. It meant so much to me that you took me in and treated me as your son. Thank you both so much.

Foreword
by Drew Blackston

When I was young, I always wanted to be an astronaut. I would lie in bed at night and dream of blasting off from Kennedy Space Center and rocketing to the stars.

Some of my early heroes were Neil Armstrong, Buzz Aldrin, Jim Lovell and John Glenn. These men were modern-day explorers. The Christopher Columbuses of our day. On clear Kentucky nights, I would grab a blanket and head to the backyard for a front row seat to the best light show this side of the galaxy. Closing my eyes, I would find myself in the cockpit of the Space Shuttle Discovery. The engines would start to roar, and I would be lifted off the ground, hurtling toward the great unknown.

Needless to say, I was a bit obsessed. I devoured any reading material I could find on space flight and constellations. My nights were filled with great discovery — from astronauts to cosmonauts. Nothing was off limits. My parents saw this desire in my heart. They even sent me to Space Camp in Huntsville, Alabama… Twice! But then something happened. I began growing up. My childhood dreams of flying through the stratosphere and landing among the constellations began to fade away. I discovered that science and calculus were less than desirable courses to me. Plus, I tended to get sick riding in the back seat of a car. After a while, it was clear that

Commander Drew Blackston was just not going to happen. The closest I would get to a space flight would be the "Mission Space" ride at Walt Disney World.

As I moved from high school to college, my dreams of space flight were replaced by a new dream — playing catcher for the Chicago Cubs. As you can see, that dream didn't work out either.

A New Dream

I now have a new dream. It's called, "The Retirement Wealth Dream." This time, my dreams are coming true. I am blessed with the opportunity to help individuals and families with their dreams of living a prosperous and abundant life in retirement. With each passing day, new clients entrust our firm with their dreams of a secure and prosperous retirement. Together, we work to develop and implement a plan that will bring their dreams to fruition for the next 20, 30 or 40 years.

As we grow older, we tend to lose sight of dreaming. The hustle and bustle of everyday life can dampen our imagination, pushing the magic of dreams further and further away. Punching the time clock and racing for the weekend becomes our end game until, before you know it, 30 years have passed and retirement starts to loom large on our horizons.

Start Dreaming Again

Why not start dreaming again? Don't let your imagination fade away with the passing of time.

Walt Disney put it this way: "All our dreams can come true if we have the courage to pursue them."

Age is not a factor when it comes to dreaming. Colonel Harland Sanders, of Kentucky Fried Chicken fame, started the first KFC at age 65!

Let's start pursuing those dreams together. Where do you see yourself in your retirement? Every day I meet with individuals and families who have retired (or will retire soon), and I always ask, "What are your dreams?" They could be traveling the world, spending more time with the grandchildren, starting a new venture or maybe volunteering time to help others. Whatever the dream, nothing is too small or too big. Age is just a number, and from my dreams of becoming an astronaut to your dreams of a prosperous retirement, I encourage you to expand your horizons. Look beyond yourself and seek new ventures. Retirement is an incredible journey. Together, dear reader, I believe we can accomplish whatever we set our hearts to.

~Drew

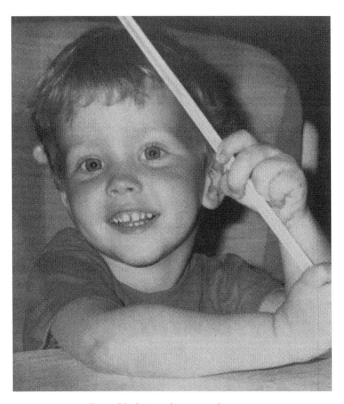

Drew Blackston, the young dreamer.

Preface

et's clarify something right away about the title of this book. Elephants rarely bite people. They are herbivores, which is to say they eat plants — lots of plants. An adult elephant can pack away up to 500 pounds of grass, leaves and tree bark per day. But, thankfully, they are not particularly interested in chewing on your arm!

My son, Drew, and I conduct several pro bono educational workshops on retirement and wealth management each year. One of the questions I like to ask the audience is: "How many here have been bitten by an elephant?"

Of course, no hands go up.

"Now, how many have been bitten by a mosquito?"

Every hand goes up.

I mean, after all, who hasn't been bitten by a mosquito? Right?

I will then point out how dangerous the mosquito is to us humans. According to the World Health Organization, this tiny insect is the deadliest animal in the world. The WHO says mosquito bites kill more than 1 million people per year. Around the globe, a child dies from malaria (a mosquito-borne disease) every 30 seconds.[1]

In Lake County, Florida, where our families work and live, mosquitos would be a bigger problem if it weren't for those fogging trucks that visit our neighborhoods in the evenings between April and December (thanks, guys). In some parts of the world, however, people have no choice but to suffer through it.

---

[1] World Health Organization. January 2016. "Malaria Fact Sheet." http://www.who.int/mediacentre/factsheets/fs094/en/.

So, what does all that have to do with managing your financial resources so that you have can have a worry-free retirement? The biggest threats to your financial security are the little things that sneak up and sting you, not some cataclysmic event you will see on the evening news. You may have saved diligently and invested wisely for years to acquire a nest egg that you hope will sustain you in your golden years, only to see those resources eaten away by scores of unforeseen small disasters for which you didn't prepare. We will discuss some of those in this book: overtaxation, overexposure to market risk, hidden fees, bad financial advice, health care issues and others — and show you how an ounce of prevention is worth a pound of cure to keep you healthy, financially, at a time when you need your money the most.

I hope you didn't buy this book expecting to find the latest and greatest stock tip. Or how to cash in on the next Apple or Google. If you did, see me personally, and I will make sure you get a refund. No one knows the future. If someone in the financial advisory profession pretends to know what the future holds, he or she is being less than honest. The closest thing I have to a crystal ball is a snow globe someone gave me one year for Christmas, and it isn't saying anything.

Neither will this book contain any get-rich-quick schemes or too-good-to-be-true investment strategies. What you will find here are perhaps some new ways of looking at old problems, and some fresh answers to the age-old question for those approaching retirement: "How can I make sure my assets last as long as I do?" You will read about financial strategies that work and are consistent with the times in which we live. You will read true-life experiences of how, with just a little planning, you can avoid those "mosquito bites" that could turn into open sores and threaten your financial well-being.

I invite you to have an open mind, too. Some of the concepts you will see in this book may be new and unfamiliar to you. That doesn't mean they aren't worthy of consideration. Everything I have ever learned was new to me at one time or another. Please follow the logic all the way through before deciding. That's all I ask. A professor once asked a group of freshmen students, "If something you thought was true wasn't true, when would you want to know it?" If you are the type of person who responds, "As soon as possible!" then you will probably enjoy the rest of this book.

"Why This Book; Why Now?"

This book has been inside me for about a decade now, itching to get out. Over the years, I have come to have strong opinions about money — the right way to save it, invest it and, perhaps most important of all, preserve it for distribution when you need it the most. I have formed some of these opinions through education, but most of them through experience. I have witnessed fortunes lost by individuals who weren't willing to change with the times. I have seen the hardships incurred by others who just let life happen to them and failed to plan. I have seen others follow the errant financial advice of well-meaning friends and relatives, and end up losing large chunks of money in the process. I have seen other folks get to the very cusp of retirement, only to be forced back into the workplace because a stock market crash swept away their savings.

Some of these "war stories," as Drew calls them, have happy endings. In fact, many of them do. You will hear some of them if you continue reading. They are about real people whose lives were changed for the better after they adjusted their investments to match their age, goals and retirement horizons. We have changed their names to protect their privacy, but the stories actually happened.

Writing this book has been a kind of catharsis for me, too. In the process of organizing my thoughts for you here, I have had to focus them with laser beam intensity. Some of the foundational truths about investing and wealth management you will read about here are not my property or even my ideas. They are "investing truths," because they proved reliable under test. When a wealth-management concept enables an ordinary investor to accomplish his or her goals despite what happens on Wall Street, in China or the Middle East, and in spite of what Congress does or doesn't do, then that strategy has earned a "this works" medal from me and can be called an investing truth.

You will also see a few "investing myths" candidly exposed for what they are in the following pages. I cannot apologize for the forthrightness and frankness with which I will dispatch some of these false notions. After all, the truth has a right to be heard, and its opposite must be exposed for the sham it is and asked to leave the room. Myths are fine for fairy tales and ancient Greek tragedies, but putting faith in them with your hard-earned money can be "hazardous to your wealth" in today's financial landscape.

Finally, you will see that I have nothing to sell here. Nothing to promote. No agenda. No ax to grind. No program to push. I will be as candid as possible in presenting accurate information and sound, basic education designed to enhance your financial position in the days ahead. Oh yes! We may have some fun in the process, too. We usually do.

The Emotions of Dealing With Money

"Worrying is like a rocking chair. It gives you something to do but it doesn't get you anywhere." ~ Anonymous

I can think of no abstract thing that generates more raw emotion than money. People rejoice in the acquisition of it, and mourn the loss of it. They angst over what to do with it once they have it, and measure their worth by how much of it they possess.

I saw a clever bumper sticker the other day that said: "Money can't buy you happiness, but it's more comfortable to cry in a Mercedes than on a bicycle." I suppose that is true.

Because of the volatility of the stock market, many investors are riding an emotional roller coaster. What has always been the mantra of successful investing? "Buy low, sell high," right? And while we know that to be true, when our emotions get in the way, it can cause us to do the exact opposite. Here's an example of the emotions some investors go through, especially the do-it-yourselfers who think they can "time" the market:

The Plunge — The market is moving steadily upward. We decide this is a trend. Our mood is hopeful. When the trend continues, we decide to get in while the getting is good. We take the plunge and buy XYZ at $50 per share. The emotion here is a little bit of greed mixed with confidence.

The Ride Up — We check the next day, and it is up $2. Wow! We are pretty savvy! We've already made money! A week goes by. Then two weeks. We are still climbing. We look at how much money we are making and begin thinking of all the things it will buy. The mood here is one of euphoria. We are exhilarated. This will go on forever, we tell ourselves. We should have gotten in sooner!

Reaching the Pinnacle — This is the riskiest point in our emotional journey, but we don't know it. This is the high point at which we should sell, only we have no way of knowing it. All markets run in cycles, but we don't want to acknowledge that fact. We are over the moon with joy. We try to resist the urge to boast of our investing prowess, but sometimes we just can't help letting our pals know that we have "done quite well in the market."

The Ride Down — Wait a minute! Share prices are falling! For the first time, our investment is losing money. This must just be a hiccup. A glitch. We tell ourselves these things just happen from time to time. But the truth is, we are a little worried. A little voice in the back of our minds tells us that we should sell now and take profits on the investment. But a louder voice says, "This is just a break in the action. Hang on! That's the smart thing to do. This will turn around. I just have a feeling." The emotions here are hope mixed with concern.

Oh, no! The slide continues the next day. And the next. Very quickly, share prices are below our entry point. The emotion now is fear mixed with regret. We should have bailed out when we had a chance. A feeling of depression and desperation sets in.

The Retreat — With a lump in our throat, we sell all shares of XYZ. There go our dreams of an early retirement right down the drain. We have just lost half of what we invested. We feel defeated. When our friends mention investing, we change the subject. We are too embarrassed to tell them about the disaster. We are through with investing forever! Sure, we have locked in our losses, but that is better than losing everything, we tell ourselves.

The Return — Then an odd thing happens. The market has bottomed out and is now showing signs of life! Our old stock XYZ is moving back up the charts. Maybe we were right after all; we just didn't follow it through. Maybe we should get back in. Now, with half of our original investment, we decide to give it another go.

Full Circle — Like the market, our emotions have come full circle. Hope, confidence, euphoria, doubt, concern, fear, desperation and back to hope.

According to Wall Street lore, when the great stock market crash of 1929 hit, and people lost fortunes overnight, some panic-stricken speculators were so overwrought they jumped out of skyscraper windows to their sudden death. Blame it on temporary insanity brought on by going from filthy rich to dirt poor in one day.

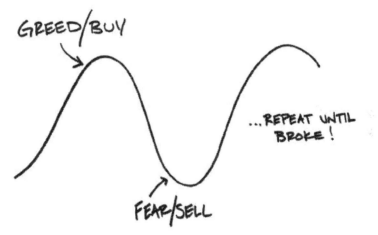

How about you? Have you ever endured a sleepless night over money? Ever worn a path in your carpet, pacing the floors back and forth, thinking about an investment or some other situation involving your personal finances? If you have, don't feel like the Lone Ranger. I talk to a lot of people, and it is a common phenomenon.

> "...72 percent of Americans reported feeling some stress over money, and 22 percent said the stress was extreme."

Each year the American Psychological Association takes a survey called, "Stress in America — Paying With Our Health." As the title of the survey implies, stress over money can make us physically sick. The 2014 study revealed that 72 percent of Americans reported feeling some stress over money, and 22 percent said the stress was extreme.[2]

According to the APA, not only can this kind of stress negatively impact our health, it can also damage our relationships with those we love. Money problems are a major source of conflict between spouses. Like the clever comic strip Maxine quipped: "Most stress is caused by three things: money, family and family with no money."

Seeking Professional Help

When you have physical problems, failure to consult a medical professional can be hazardous to your health. Failure to consult the right financial professional with money issues and concerns can be hazardous to your wealth! The APA survey suggests that if you experience money stress, you should talk to someone. Don't keep it bottled up inside. I suggest you find someone whom you can (a) trust, and someone who can (b) give you good advice. The trust factor is important. You have to know that the other person is not working from a profit motive. They must have your best interests at heart, and not their own. Notice, I didn't say that the person you go to for advice would necessarily offer it without charge. If that were the case, the medical, legal and financial professions would be out of business. But they must not be *motivated* by profit. (We will

---

[2] American Psychological Association. Feb. 4, 2015. "American Psychological Association Survey Shows Money Stress Weighing on American's Health Nationwide." http://www.apa.org/news/press/releases/2015/02/money-stress.aspx.

talk more about that later, and you will see the word "fiduciary" pop up quite a bit.) Life would have turned out differently for my mother had she and my father taken that path.

My Parents' Story

My father, Clifford Blackston, died at age 65 from cancer brought on by toxic exposure to asbestos, better known as Mesothelioma. He worked for the railroad. My father was no job hopper. After serving nine years in the military, he signed on with the railroad and stayed there for the rest of his working life. In those days, asbestos was used to insulate everything from locomotive brakes to the lining of passenger cars. Railroad workers were particularly at risk. People just didn't know how dangerous the fibrous material was. My father was probably a young man in the prime of life when the tiny fibers first began invading his lungs, forming the scar tissue that later killed him.

Dad retired when he was 62 and my mother, Sue, was 59. My father sometimes complained of shortness of breath but passed it off as nothing that warranted a doctor's visit. One day while playing golf, my father sneezed, and said it felt as if he had broken a rib. His coughing worsened. He passed away a year later.

My father was an intelligent man, and very independent — a do-it-yourself type who was usually quite good at figuring things out. To some extent, that was part of the problem. By his calculations, his railroad pension, combined with his Social Security (and eventually hers) would allow them to retire in relative comfort. But Dad did not know what he didn't know. For whatever reason, my parents never sought financial counseling or help to plan their retirement. My father would never know that, upon his death, his pension would go to zero, and the only income my mother would have would be his Social Security. No one told him he should have opted for a survivor's benefit on his pension plan. Such a provision would have protected my mother financially for the rest of her life. If anyone did discuss this provision with him, they must not have made it crystal clear to him. Otherwise, I feel sure he would have chosen it. As it turned out, Mom would eventually have to leave the family home and move into a small apartment.

I watched my mother struggle financially. I was a banker when my dad passed away. You may wonder why I didn't advise them on retirement, but as a banker I only knew about loaning money, not retirement strategies. I remember what an important day it was when Mother's monthly check arrived in the mail. I watched her pay the household bills in order of priority and calculate what was left. It was barely enough to get her by. She would put on a cheerful face and say, "There is always too much month and never enough money."

At age 19, I entered the adult workforce as a bank teller. My first job was wrapping coins at a bank where I would later become vice president. As I matured and gained more experience in the world of finance, I saw very clearly the mistakes my parents had made and what it had cost them. Today, when people ask me why I chose to become a financial advisor, I explain to them that it affected me deeply to see my mother's life affected so negatively because she and my father hadn't planned. My goal in working with people preparing for retirement is to prevent them from having to go through what she went through. You can't un-ring a bell or cry over spilled milk, but what a difference just a little financial planning would have made in the lives of my parents.

David Blackston as a young boy.

Sue, left, and Clifford Blackston.

CHAPTER TWO

Getting the "Big Picture" Through Holistic Planning

"Not everything that can be counted counts, and not everything that counts can be counted." ~ Albert Einstein

When it comes to planning our financial future, we have to think "big picture." Get the overall scope of things.

To illustrate what I mean by "getting the big picture," consider what happened to the motion picture industry after World War II. When the war ended in 1945, there were fewer than 10,000 television "sets" (that's what we called them back then) in America. They were toys for the rich. The first mass-production TVs were made by RCA in the late 1940s and cost $352 — about one-fourth of the price of a new automobile in those days. TVs were not flying off the shelves. For one thing, they cost too much. For another, there wasn't too much to watch on them. But programming improved as prices came down. Suddenly, Americans just couldn't get enough TV. Despite their grainy images and the unpredictable reception, by 1950, there were 6 million televisions in American living rooms. That figure soared to 60 million by 1960. The small picture (TV) was in and the big picture (movie theatre) was out. Many baby boomers still remember the grainy, black and white shows, like "The Honeymooners" and "I Love Lucy." Sensing their share of the entertainment market was slipping, Hollywood fought back with something television couldn't offer — color and wide screens. Suddenly, the "big picture" was making a comeback. Epic blockbusters like "The Robe" and "Ben-Hur" were shot using special wide-angle lenses that required wall-to-wall rectangular screens. The effect was to make you feel like you were there!

"Getting the big picture when it comes to financial planning simply means getting every aspect of your financial life in the picture."

Eventually, when TV networks began airing these "old" movies, they found the action wouldn't fit the small, square television screens. TV producers began using a technique called "pan-and-scan," or cropping the sides of the original widescreen image, and focusing on what the pan-and-scan editors considered to be the shot's most important aspect. In the 1959 epic "Ben-Hur," for example, the original movie showed Charlton Heston driving four heaving horses around the pylons in the famous chariot race scene. On television, the viewer sees only two chariots. In the original version, you see four more competing chariots in the same shot, with thousands of cheering Roman spectators in the background. The television version gives the impression of the scene, but critics said it failed to convey its depth and grandeur. Movie people filed lawsuits against television networks for what they said was a "mutilation" of their artistic work.

Getting the big picture when it comes to financial planning simply means getting every aspect of your financial life in the picture. A competent financial planner will never recommend a course of action without knowing the "full picture," so to speak, so that every area of the client's life is taken into full consideration. This is why it is called "holistic" financial planning. In medicine, doctors using the holistic approach strive not to cause an ailment in the process of curing another.

All you have to do is listen to the long list of possible side effects during the pill commercials on television to know that when we swallow medicine to help one condition, it may very well cause another ailment to appear. Holistic medical practitioners treat the whole body, not just an organ here or a limb there. They work on the premise that the body is one interconnected biological wonder that can be put out of its natural synchrony quite easily. A drug may be potent enough to banish back pain, for example, but it may also cause liver problems. A pill to help the liver may damage the heart.

What if a financial plan had you investing so much of your paycheck into a savings plan that it allowed you no vacations, or forced you to work three jobs? You would burn out after a while, wouldn't you? What is it worth to have all that money saved up if you are too bent and broken to enjoy it when you retire? Someone missed getting the "big picture," didn't they?

One man who eventually became a client of Blackston Financial Advisory Group told me that for the past 15 years he had earned only $14,000 per year. Something didn't add up. How could he wear such expensive clothes and drive a new SUV if his earnings were below the poverty line? As it turns out, a well-meaning accountant had urged him to set up a corporation and pay himself very little in salary, and let the bulk of the money come from the corporation in the way of dividends. That would reduce his personal income tax liabilities dramatically. Good move, right? Not when you saw the "big picture." When he reached Social Security age, the man wondered why the amount he stood to collect each month was so much lower than that of his peers. It was because he had paid hardly anything into the system! Social Security, for all that it is and all that it may not be, is still a lifetime monthly income stream with an adjustment for inflation. Sometimes solving one problem begets another. A holistic approach to financial planning would have prevented that.

In medicine, holism is the theory that you should treat the whole person, not just isolated symptoms. In other words, if someone complains of a bad back to a doctor who practices holistic medicine, that doctor would not just dash off a prescription for pain pills. Treating the whole person would require finding the root of the problem and trying to correct it. Did the patient lift something heavy and pull a muscle? Did the patient fall? How long has the problem persisted? Is a change in the patient's routine or environment warranted? If the doctor did prescribe medication or a course of treatment, he or she would first determine what other drugs the patient was taking. The idea behind holistic medicine is that all the parts of the body are interconnected. The brain does not work independent of the heart, and the skeletal system does not exist independently from the nervous system. The whole is a collection of all of its parts, and, from a medical perspective, one thing affects everything else and vice versa. It's that way with our financial picture, too.

How do you get the "big picture" of your finances? You start by sitting down with a competent advisor who knows how to discern from you what you want out of life.

You don't start with figures. You start with dreams.

Where do you see yourself when you retire? Still at home, or traveling?

What do you see yourself doing? Playing with the grandchildren, or scaling mountains and learning to sail?

Also, what are your intentions regarding legacy? How much of your estate do you wish to leave behind to those you love?

One couple I know of had a motor home that was a palace inside. The Miami Dolphins could have lived inside this place. When they parked this dude, the roof popped up in two places and the walls expanded. There were two high-definition TVs and a hot tub inside. The bumper sticker on the back of the bus read, "We are spending our children's inheritance." I think they meant every word of it.

On the other hand, I know of some couples who feel duty bound to use their wealth to make a mark in the world, starting with their family. For some people, their children come first, and then the grandchildren. Others feel that their children are all set financially, so they want to pass on as much of their wealth as possible to their grandchildren.

Still others are charitably minded. Perhaps they wish to use their wealth to help children in foreign countries where living conditions are not as good as those in America. Others may want to help fight a disease that has somehow personally affected their family. Still others may wish to leave as much as possible to a church or a favorite charity.

I know of one woman whose heart was touched by the plight of abandoned animals. She formed a foundation with her considerable wealth to serve those ends. So it really is "different strokes for different folks" when it comes to their money and what they want it to do for them.

Holistic financial planning requires that the planner first listen carefully to the client. As my mother used to say, "God gave us two ears and one mouth for a reason." Or to quote Yogi Berra, "You can observe a lot by watching."

On the first interview with a prospective client, the holistic financial planner will usually have nothing but a legal pad, a pen and lots of questions — the typical who, what, where, when, why and how much questions. That's what Drew and

"How do you get the 'big picture' of your finances? You don't start with figures. You start with dreams."

I do, anyway. Because, if those basic areas are not explored first, it is impossible to proceed effectively.

If you picked this book up to learn of specific ways you can build your wealth and preserve it, don't worry; we will get to them. But first, I wanted to establish the fact — and I hope you agree with me — that no strategy, no matter how well it is thought out or cleverly designed, is worth a tinker's damn unless it fulfills a dream. Money, when you get right down to it, is just a means by which we measure. It is an accounting tool. It's the math of wealth, not the essence of it. Real wealth has life-changing, life-enhancing power that enables us to accomplish our goals, aspirations and dreams.

The Story of Joe

From time to time, we read of millionaires who lived like tramps because money meant nothing to them. One story I can't get out of my mind is the one about Joe Temeczko, who was a Polish immigrant and former prisoner of war during World War II. He did odd jobs for people in New York City where he lived an austere life. He had no family. He lived in a very small house filled with junk he had scavenged from the streets. He roamed the neighborhoods in shabby clothes, looking for discarded items that he would repair and either sell for very little or give away. He took his meals in homeless shelters or got food to take home from charities. He would stop at the newsstands on the street and read, never buying the newspapers. When he died at age 86, he left behind $1.4 million in a bank account, which he gifted to the city of New York in a will he had rewritten the night after 9/11. The point is, wealth is an abstract unless we can be specific about what we want it to accomplish.[3]

As we discuss the nuts and bolts of some of the techniques of building and preserving wealth, I invite you to crystallize your

---

[3] Tad Friend. The New Yorker. Sept. 20, 2004. "A Handyman's Gift." http://www.newyorker.com/magazine/2004/09/20/a-handymans-gift.

thinking as to how these strategies can (a) create personal wealth, and (b) enhance your life. The second one will call for a good degree of introspection and may be more difficult than the first. You will also encounter terms with which you may be unfamiliar. I will do my best to explain what these terms mean. Financial strategies for wealth building are often merely a repositioning of assets so that they attract more in the way of returns and create less in the way of taxes. But if they are not clear to you, and if you are not comfortable with them, then it's like wearing an uncomfortable pair of shoes or reading a page from a book in a language you don't understand.

The Accumulation Phase

I'm going to go out on a limb here and say that you, dear reader, are not the same person you were 10 years ago. Don't get me wrong; of course you are the same old you. What I mean is, over time your temperament and attitudes have changed. Especially about money. When you were in high school, were you serious about your financial future? Probably not, unless you were the class nerd. We took things as they came. We didn't worry much about tomorrow. We lived in the here and now. Our hourglass was full of sand in the top half.

But when we entered the workplace and began raising families, everything changed pretty quickly, didn't it? More was at stake. We wanted the best for ourselves and our children. Even though it was still far off, we began thinking of retirement in real terms, not as some abstract eventuality for old folks.

If we worked for a company that offered a 401(k), we most likely saw the wisdom in contributing as much as we could to it — especially if the company matched a portion of it. At least, I hope that was the case. That matching money was free money! Hopefully, we put that 401(k) (or its equivalent) in the category of "untouchable" money so we could get the maximum growth out of it. Financial professionals call this the "accumulation phase" of our lives, because we are building our nest egg for the future. When we are younger, it behooves us to take more risk. I'm not talking about going to Las Vegas and putting it all on a lucky number at the roulette wheel, but we can afford to be more aggressive when we are young because time is on our side. If we are participating in a retirement savings program, such as a 401(k), we are protected by the concept of something called "dollar cost averaging," too.

Dollar Cost Averaging

Dollar cost averaging is an investing technique that reduces market risk through regularly and systematically investing in the stock market, purchasing securities at pre-determined intervals with set amounts of capital. You have probably benefited from the concept, even if you didn't know it existed. Let me explain. Say you work for BIG Corporation and a portion of each paycheck goes into your 401(k). The custodian of your retirement account will probably use that contribution to buy shares in a mutual fund. When the market is down, that is not a bad thing if you are making regular contributions. Why? Because the shares are cheaper, and the dollar amount of your contribution buys more shares. When the market trends upward, those cheaper shares will gain in value. Either way the market swings, you are protected. But again, the key is regular, steady investing with a pre-determined amount.

Time is on the side of younger investors if they are patient and consistent. Dollar cost averaging allows them to accumulate wealth, spreading out the cost basis over several years.

The Preservation and Distribution Phase

When do we move from the *accumulation* phase of our financial lives to the *preservation and distribution* phase? Typically, it is when we stop working and begin to live off what we have accumulated.

The idea is to work hard, save as much as possible and invest wisely. If we have done that, we should have amassed a comfortable "nest egg" for our golden years of retirement. Do we still want our assets to grow? Sure we do! But not at the risk of losing what we have accumulated. Translation — we are (or should be) more conservative in this phase. Just as dollar cost averaging was our protection when we were in the accumulation phase, something called *reverse* dollar cost averaging can threaten our financial security in our later years.

Reverse Dollar Cost Averaging

In a way, it's a bit ironic that what helps us in our younger investing years could come back to bite us in our financial posteriors when we retire. Let's say you have quit your job at the BIG Corporation. The paychecks are gone, and with them, the contributions to your employer-sponsored 401(k) plan. You are in full retirement. The "money river" is now flowing the other way. Instead of contributing to a fund, you must begin withdrawing from it. Essentially, you are replacing the paycheck you used to receive with drawdowns from your savings and investments. Those workplace resources (your paycheck) were renewable as long as you were working. Now, you are depending on nonrenewable resources to meet your basic expenses.

Here's where *reverse* dollar cost averaging comes in. When you make withdrawals from your retirement fund, you are selling shares. If you are like most folks, you must make those withdrawals with the same regularity with which you made contributions earlier. It is a given that the market will always fluctuate. When the market is down, you must sell more shares to make the same "paycheck." If we have another market crash, like the one in 2008, then the value of your account goes down dramatically. Those losses are even more disastrous when you are retired. Time is no longer on our side. You are no longer buying cheaper shares that will eventually regain value. That money is gone forever. You are depleting the account at a faster rate during a market downturn and are not able to recover when the market rebounds.

The Rule of 100

It is not unusual for me to be sitting across the table from someone who is telling me they want to retire in five years, yet their portfolio is completely at risk in the stock market, where half of it could vanish virtually overnight. That's what I mean about their investments not matching their stated purpose for their money.

One rule of thumb that is helpful in correcting this risk imbalance is the "Rule of 100." The concept is pretty straightforward. Take your age, and subtract it from 100. That is approximately the percentage of your investable assets you should have at risk. The rest you should have invested where you cannot lose it.

Remember, the Rule of 100 is a "rule of thumb." Only a guideline. Risk tolerances vary, as do individual circumstances. But staying within the framework of this investing principle will protect the assets of the retiree (and soon-to-be retired). It will also serve to coax younger investors, who have more time on their side, to be more aggressive. Unfortunately, some young people squander wealth-building opportunities. How would the Rule of 100 apply to them? A 25-year-old investor should have approximately 75 percent of his or her assets at risk in long-term securities with real growth potential, and 25 percent in a safe, liquid emergency fund.

CHAPTER THREE

Passing the Financial Torch

"I am very concerned about the millions of baby boomers who are counting on the stock market to deliver them a safe, sound, long retirement. I am afraid the baby boomers who are counting on the stock market are in trouble." ~ Robert Kiyosaki

If you hear thundering hooves approaching, that's no buffalo herd — it is the great 21st century retirement stampede!

Demographers tell us that approximately 10,000 baby boomers are turning 65 every day, quitting their jobs, signing up for Medicare and plugging into Social Security. When I first heard that statistic, I couldn't help but think of nearby (to us, anyway) Raymond James Stadium, where the Tampa Bay Buccaneers play football. That stadium holds close to 70,000 people. Every week, that many Americans are

> *10,000 baby boomers turn 65 EVERY DAY*

retiring. Spread out over a year, that's nearly 4 million people! You can just imagine what an impact that is having on the nation.[4]

To officially qualify to be a "baby boomer" your birth year has to have been between 1946 and 1964. Those years saw a tremendous increase in the birth rate in America. Soldiers who went to war in World War II were children of the Great Depression. When they returned, they did what came naturally — found jobs, got married, started families and began producing and consuming like no other generation in history. The children of these families grew up in a different world than the one their parents had experienced, and they would go on to change the social and economic fabric of the nation.

So now, this generation that put human footprints on the moon, invented rock 'n' roll and first used the credit card is starting to retire, ready or not. Some of those in this retirement stampede have their act together and know exactly how much they need to live on every month. Some have saved adequately and can live in relative comfort with the assurance they won't run out of money in their old age. But, according to most surveys, these prudent planners are in the minority, far outnumbered by those who overspent, undersaved and didn't plan properly.

"Are You Better Off Than Your Parents?"

How would you answer this question: "When it comes to personal wealth, are you better off than your parents' generation?"

This is one of the topics we frequently discuss in the seminars Drew and I conduct and on our radio show.

One of the most thorough and well-researched books I have read on this subject is "Baby Boomers and Their Parents, Surprising

---

[4] Glenn Kessler. The Washington Post. July 24, 2014. "Fact Checker: Do 10,000 baby boomers retire every day?" https://www.washingtonpost.com/blogs/fact-checker/wp/2014/07/24/do-10000-baby-boomers-retire-every-day.

Findings About Their Lifestyles, Mindsets, and Well-Being," written by George P. Moschis, Ph.D, and Anil Mathur, Ph.D. They surveyed thousands of people and arrived at some surprising conclusions.

When it comes to health, baby boomers are living longer than the generations that preceded us, but are we in as good health as they? Moschis and Mathur say no. As odd as it may seem, boomers are more preoccupied with health than their parents' generation, and are all about diet and exercise on the face of it, but compared with adults the same age 20 years ago, they weigh more and have more ailments. They say part of the problem is "time pressure." I can vouch for that. We seem chained to our devices (laptops, smartphones, tablets). Because we **can** communicate instantly, we feel as if we **must** communicate instantly. The boom generation gets things done, all right, but probably doesn't take as much downtime as it needs. Then when we read paragraphs like this about stress, we start to stress out that we are stressed out, right?

The book said that one of the fears weighing on the minds of today's baby boomers is old age. Not necessarily getting older chronologically; everyone expects that eventuality. Boomers are concerned with the fear of, as the book puts it, "the inability to keep their independence and becoming a burden on younger relatives."

In other words, living too long and running out of money.

What's ironic is boomers have earned more money, even accounting for inflation, than any other previous generation. So what's the problem?

For one thing, there has been a dramatic shift in the support structure for aging Americans. Somewhere in the 1980s, the defined benefit pension plan, which was the cornerstone of most retirement plans, began to disappear. The words "defined benefit" meant your pension would be permanent and dependable. You worked for BIG Corporation for 30 to 40 years and received a gold watch and a lifetime paycheck. For the most part, those days are gone. Nowadays, you are given a defined *contribution* savings plan. The "contribution," by the way, comes from you. If you are lucky, your employer contributes a separate portion to the plan; contributing "matching funds" that match what you put in *up to a point.*

These plans typically invest in mutual funds, which makes them subject to the ebb and flow of the stock market. If workers don't actively participate in the program, then they won't receive the benefits of the program. If the stock market crashes at the wrong time (close to retirement) the participant will not have time to recover from the hit. That's a lot to worry about for a retiring baby boomer.

OK, so you can't necessarily rely on a pension to keep you up in retirement. What about Social Security?

Good question. The Social Security Administration informs us that this stampede of retiring baby boomers will put a serious burden on the program. In the SSA's 2013 report, it predicted that "By 2015, almost 33 percent of our workforce, including 48 percent of our supervisors, will be eligible to retire. In FY [fiscal year] 2011, we lost more than 4,000 employees due to retirement and other reasons. We expect this trend to continue. During this same timeframe, the baby boomer retirement wave continues to have a significant effect on our workloads."[5]

Every year Americans receive (or are given access to via the web) a report from the Social Security Administration that provides a plethora of information about their SS account. How much they have earned over their lifetime so far. How much they stand to receive each month when they retire. That sort of thing. On the front page of this report is an ominous warning, however, that should be a sobering awakening for anyone who thinks that they can trust the government to take care of them:

[5] Social Security Administration. 2013. "Fiscal Year 2013 Annual Performance Plan and Revised Final FY 2012 APP." https://www.ssa.gov/agency/performance/2013/.

"**About Social Security's future...** Social Security is a compact between generations. Since 1935, America has kept the promise of security for its workers and their families. Now, however, the Social
Security system is facing serious financial problems, and action is
needed soon to make sure the system will be sound when today's
younger workers are ready for retirement. Without changes, in 2033
the Social Security Trust Fund will be able to pay only about 77 cents
for each dollar of scheduled benefits.* We need to resolve these issues
soon to make sure Social Security continues to provide a foundation of
protection for future generations.

*These estimates are based on the intermediate assumptions from the
Social Security Trustees' Annual Report to the Congress." [6]

Let's not forget that the baby boomer retirement stampede will
put pressure on the Medicare system as well. Sure, maybe Congress
will pass legislation fixing all of this, or part of it. But when I take
my informal surveys, confidence in government solutions seems to
be in short supply.

Before we get off the subject, here are some troubling statistics
from the 2013 Government Accountability Office "Survey of Consumer Finances":

- **48 percent** – Americans with some retirement savings
- **29 percent** – Americans with no defined benefit plan or retirement savings
- **23 percent** – Americans with a defined benefit plan but no
retirement savings

Look at the second bullet point. The GAO found that of that
percentage, 65 percent either didn't own their own home or still
owed on a mortgage. As far as how poorly some baby boomers are
prepared for retirement, here is a quote from the report:

---

[6] Social Security Administration. 2016. "Your Social Security Statement."
https://www.ssa.gov/myaccount/SSA-7005-OL.pdf.

"The average profile of a baby boomer in the 29% shows they have just $1,000 in financial assets, annual income of just $18,932, and a net worth of only $34,760. Those are terrifying statistics that imply a substantial number of boomers will be relying on Social Security to fuel their retirement. This is concerning because the Social Security's Old-Age, Survivors and Disability Trust could be facing up to a 23% benefits cut by 2033 if Congress can't figure out a way to boost revenue, cut expenses, or enact some combination of the two."[7]

The national debt is another scary specter for retiring baby boomers (and for their children). The government is in the habit of spending more than it collects in revenue — henceforth, the national debt.

If you are ever in New York City, walk to the intersection of West 44th Street and Avenue of the Americas, and you will see a billboard-sized display of the National Debt Clock. I don't know how they do it, but it is purportedly an up-to-the-second calculation of how much our nation owes. The numbers on the right side of the figure are just a blur, but it's somewhere in the neighborhood of $18 trillion as I write this in March 2016. You don't have to go all the way to New York to see it. Just visit the website www.usdebtclock.org and see for yourself. That's your money disappearing.

The problem with a number as vast as a trillion is we can't wrap our minds around it. Trillion rhymes with billion and million, so it is easy to miss the significance of an $18 trillion national debt. To put it into some perspective, a million is a thousand thousands. A billion is a thousand million. Still doesn't grab you? How about this. A million seconds are equal to 11.5 days. A billion seconds are equal to 31.5 years. A trillion seconds make up 31,000 years.

---

[7] Government Accountability Office. May 2015. "Most Households Approaching Retirement Have Low Savings." United States Government Accountability Office Report to the Ranking Member, Subcommittee on Primary Health and Retirement Security, Committee on Health, Education, Labor and Pensions, U.S. Senate. Analysis of 2013 Survey of Consumer Finances data. GAO 15-419.

We get to the point where we just throw up our hands and say it's too much for us to comprehend. The point is, every man, woman and child currently alive and even those of future generations will be affected by this red ink. If the government were a business, like Wal-Mart or Apple, it would have been bankrupt a long time ago. Unlike corporations, the government has a fallback position no business has. The government can print money.

Unfunded liabilities — that's another scary phrase for Americans, or, at least, it should be. At the bottom of the before-mentioned National Debt Clock on its dedicated website (www.usdebtclock.org), you will see a box labeled "US Unfunded Liabilities." As I write this, that figure is around $100 trillion, give or take a trillion. What are unfunded liabilities? It's what the nation owes when you throw in Social Security, Medicare and all the other entitlement programs. Entitlements are promises the government makes to provide services with money it expects to have in the future. To put it in everyday terms, it would be the same as if you wrote a check for the rent with no money in the bank, anticipating that someone who owes you money will pay you to cover it. Unfunded liabilities are all of the government programs that pay for services Uncle Sam renders based on borrowed money. Is it any wonder that Americans who understand the significance of these figures feel a bit insecure these days? Who is going to pay for all of this? You and, most likely, your children and grandchildren.

If you balance your checkbook every month, then this might put it in terms you can easily grasp. We are going to leave off some zeroes here, but you get the idea of what Uncle Sam's personal balance sheet looks like with things as they stand now.

INCOME	$28,000
EXPENSES	$34,000
DEBT	$180,000
FUTURE EXPENSES	$1,260,000

So, let's see now. Uncle Sam makes $28,000 per year. He spends $34,000 annually. He is in debt to the tune of $180,000. So much interest is accruing that he can't pay off the debt. Future liabilities total more than $1.2 million. If you were a bank, would you lend him money? My point is there was a time when the future was rock solid. Not anymore.

Concern for Future Generations

So, again. Do you think your children will have it better than you when they retire? Usually, when we throw that question out for discussion at a client event, the response is 50/50. Half say yes, the other half no.

But when we ask, "How many of you think your grandchildren are going to be better off than you in retirement?" only one fourth of the hands in the room go up. Why?

Let's tick off some positives for the grandkids: Better access to education. Advances in science. They will have career opportunities in specialized fields, such as technology and health care, and careers in fields we cannot yet imagine. But the overriding negative that is going to hold back the generations to come is debt. Not just the national indebtedness this generation is packing on their backs, but crippling personal debt. If debt were a drug, the entire nation seems to be high on the stuff.

Do you think your children will have it better than you when they retire?

According to NerdWallet.com, a website that tracks personal debt, American consumers are deep in debt, and it's getting worse every year. The level of debt for 2015, for example, was 5.9 percent higher than it was for 2014.

NerdWallet lists the following alarming statistics, current as of October 2015:[8]

- Average credit card debt: $16,140
- Average mortgage debt: $155,361
- Average student loan debt: $31,946
- Total owed by American consumers: $11.85 trillion (up 1.4 percent from 2014)
- Total credit card debt owed by American consumers: $918.5 billion
- Total mortgage debt held by Americans: $809 trillion
- Total student loan debt in America: $1.19 trillion

Wow! How can young families ever begin to save or invest dragging around that kind of ball and chain? According to an October 2014 article in U.S. News and World Report, students enter the workforce having no clue as to how long it will take them to dig out from under their student loan debt. The article stated: "The standard repayment plan for federal student loans puts borrowers on a 10-year track to pay off their debt, but research has shown the average bachelor's degree holder takes 21 years to pay off his or her loans. Under federal-income-based repayment options, the remaining debt is forgiven after 20 years."[9]

Personally, I agree with the proverb: "Good people leave an inheritance to their grandchildren." Despite the current debt trends, I am convinced we can help the next generations. I'm not just talking about leaving them wads of cash, either. Here are a few things I recommend to audiences when I speak:

---

[8] Erin El Issa. NerdWallet. 2015. "2015 American Household Credit Card Debt Study. https://www.nerdwallet.com/blog/credit-card-data/average-credit-card-debt-household/.

[9] Allie Bidwell. Oct. 7, 2014. "Student Loan Expectations: Myth vs. Reality." http://www.usnews.com/news/blogs/data-mine/2014/10/07/student-loan-expectations-myth-vs-reality.

- Talk to your kids and grandkids about investing. Even the smallest amount of money invested monthly is a good start. Most people think you need to have large sums of money to invest. That's not true. Warren Buffet started with a $200 investment, and look at him now. He was worth some $72.3 billion at last count. Everyone starts somewhere. Teach them that consistency is the key.

- Why not set up separate investing accounts for the young people? Get them interested in the principles of saving and investing. You may wish to add money to these accounts periodically, but that is your call. The main thing is to help them learn saving, budgeting and the power of investing.

- Buy life insurance with your kids and grandkids as beneficiaries. It is a simple way to make sure that money is passed on to kids or grandkids when you pass away. If you have children or grandchildren who you think would spend the proceeds foolishly, most life insurance companies allow for restricted beneficiaries on their policies. This will allow you to manage how death benefits are paid out to the different beneficiaries. If you want to be more detailed, set up a trust with an attorney.

In our family, we have always had the motto, "Plan for the worst and pray for the best." All of the fiscal woes of our future generations won't be solved by any single act such as those listed above. But it is a good place to start.

The Three-Legged Stool

Once upon a time, financial planning consisted of the three-legged stool. This tripod was supposed to support us in retirement. It consisted of three things: Social Security, pensions and personal savings.

Well, forget about pensions. They are quickly becoming extinct. If you have one, consider yourself lucky.

Social Security? It will probably be here for baby boomers, but the way things are going there are no guarantees for the next generation.

That leaves us with personal savings. How wisely you invest that and use it can make all the difference, as the next chapters will show.

CHAPTER FOUR

A Guaranteed Income or a Maybe Income - Which Do You Want When You Retire?

"Today there are about 40 million retirees receiving benefits; by the time all the baby boomers have retired, there will be more than 72 million retirees drawing Social Security benefits." ~ Tony Snow

In my opinion, one of the most egregious mistakes people make when structuring their retirement is failing to have an income plan. Isn't that the point of planning for retirement? To make sure you don't run out of money? To make sure you will continue to have a paycheck in your golden years after you quit working your day job?

But wait a minute, Dave! I have an income plan, don't I? I have my 401(k). Isn't that for income when I retire?

It is if you are happy with a "maybe" income plan instead of a "guaranteed" income plan. Don't get me wrong. Defined contribution retirement plans, such as 401(k)s and 403(b)s and other deferred savings/investment accounts like them, are great for accumulation purposes, just not for distribution purposes. Why? Because they aren't guaranteed.

Millions of Americans learned that lesson the hard way during the financial crisis of 2008. Throughout the 1990s, they saw their retirement accounts getting fatter and fatter, thanks to a healthy economy and a roaring stock market. All boats rose on that tide, including the mutual funds in which most 401(k) contributions were invested. But when the mortgage bubble burst in 2007, and the big banks began failing in 2008, the domino effect kicked in. The tide rapidly receded, leaving many, especially older workers, high and dry. In some cases, their retirement accounts were stripped down to half of their value. One reason the crash hit older workers the hardest had to do with timing. They did not have time to wait for the tide to return. Younger workers had time on their side. They would continue working and wait for the recovery to rebuild their accounts. Older workers facing retirement had a stark choice: bite the bullet — that is, pare down their standards of living and retire on less than they had planned on — or keep working and try to rebuild their savings.

Mark and Sharon were a typical American couple looking forward to retirement. They had a date circled in 2009 when Mark would retire from his job at a large software development company. He had accumulated around $250,000 in his 401(k) retirement savings program at work, and Sharon, who had gone back to teaching school after the kids were grown and gone, had around $15,000 in hers. They figured that, with Social Security, they could retire in relative comfort.

Then the market crash of 2008 happened. They watched helplessly as their retirement savings began to evaporate. Mark lost nearly 45 percent of his savings, and Sharon nearly half of hers. By the time I met them, they were coming to terms with the idea of postponing retirement for at least four more years, and even then they were doubtful they could rebuild enough to compensate for the losses.

"We knew the money (in the 401(k)s) was in mutual funds, but we thought it was diversified enough to protect it from that big a loss," Mark said. "We saw pretty quickly that none of those funds were guaranteed."

When we sat down to examine their account statements, Mark and Sharon discovered another shocker. The fees associated with their investments within the mutual funds in their 401(k)s continued after the market faltered, further eroding their savings. They, like most folks I talk to, were unaware of the fees associated with 401(k) retirement plans — administrative fees, investment fees, individual service fees, not to mention the sales charges and maintenance fees on the mutual funds in which their assets are actually invested.

"Just Hang in There"

"But the stock market always comes back. Just hang in there."

You hear that a lot from stockbrokers after a market crash. And there is truth in that statement. Historically, the stock market has always rebounded after a crash. But those on the cusp of retirement are transitioning from accumulation to distribution. They do not have time to benefit from a market recovery (see Chapter Two — Reverse Dollar Cost Averaging).

That's what happened to Mark and Sharon. They had no place to run. If they retired, they would have to make withdrawals from their savings to pay bills and maintain their lifestyle. If they ran to the shelter of such safe havens as certificates of deposit (bank CDs) and money market accounts, they would receive little to no return on their money. What if they "doubled down," as they say in Las Vegas at the gambling tables? They could elevate their risk in an attempt to play catch-up with their market investments. The danger is obvious that they could lose what's left.

The Government's MyRA

As if sensing the people's thirst for "guaranteed" income over "maybe" income, the U.S. government is, as I write this, in the process of unveiling its own retirement program, called MyRA. It is a play on the well-known acronym, IRA, which stands for Individual Retirement Account (or Individual Retirement Arrangement, if you want to get technical). The U.S. Treasury Department is touting the program as an IRA alternative for the millions of Americans who do not have 401(k)s at work or who have chosen not to participate in them.[10]

On a refreshing note, the government promises that myRAs will have no fees or hidden charges that could eat into participants' annual returns. To participate in the program, you must earn less than $131,000 per year ($193,000 if married and filing taxes jointly). The rules are similar to other deferred savings programs. You are limited to $5,000 in contributions per year ($6,500 if you are 50 years of age or older by 2015). MyRA works on the same principle as a Roth IRA. You put in taxed dollars and make tax-free withdrawals. You can roll your myRA over into a private account at any time. In fact, you will be forced to do so when the account is 30 years old or has reached a maximum $15,000 balance — whichever comes first. Your savings ARE guaranteed, though. The program is backed by the U.S. Government, which, last time I checked, is the only entity that can legally print money.

---

[10] Melanie Hicken. CNN Money. Jan. 18, 2015. "Obama's myRA retirement accounts are now a reality." http://money.cnn.com/2015/01/18/retirement/myra-retirement-accounts.

Well, nice try, Uncle Sam, but the myRA is not the end-all-be-all to the quest for the guaranteed income retirees need. For one thing, myRA contributions will be invested solely in government bonds. MyRAs may be free of risk, but from what I read, myRA returns will be pretty paltry.

Critics of the program include Forbes magazine contributor John E. Girouard, who calls the myRA a "wolf in sheep's clothing."

"The federal government is stuck with a lot of unpopular bonds, and one sure-fire way to get rid of them is to sell them to the American public as a retirement savings vehicle," writes Girouard. "Those bonds that our government now owns are yielding low rates at a time when most experts are predicting that interest rates will be rising again. When interest rates rise, the value of a bond falls."[11]

Whatever Became of Pensions?

Would you believe there is a link between the demise of pensions and the disappearance of Studebakers? You may be a baby boomer if you ever sat behind the wheel (or in the passenger seat, for that matter) of a Studebaker.

The main problem with these cars was they were ahead of their time. They were fast, streamlined and had lots of safety features (seatbelts, for example) long before other automakers had them. But for some reason, the fickle American car-buying public just didn't like Studebakers — at least not enough to keep them in business. By the 1960s, the company was on the verge of bankruptcy. What drove the venerable old car manufacturer over the edge was — you guessed it — its pension obligations. In the boom years of the 1950s, unions forced Studebaker to give its workers better and better fringe benefits. Keep in mind, this was a time when, if you

---

[11] John E. Girouard. Forbes. Feb. 3, 2014. "Obama's MyRA Savings Plan: Wolf in Sheep's Clothing?" http://www.forbes.com/sites/investor/2014/02/03/obamas-myra-savings-plan-wolf-in-sheeps-clothing/#3708325b6530.

landed a job building automobiles, you were set for life. If you worked there for 30 or 40 years, you could expect to retire with a gold watch and a pension that guaranteed you a paycheck for the rest of your life, and for an amount close to what you made when you were working.

When American consumers started opting for foreign cars instead of Studebakers, and the company had to close up shop in 1964, the corporation had to let the secret out that it simply couldn't keep its pension promises. That news led to the discovery that other companies had been mishandling their employee pension plans, as well. Congress got involved after NBC News aired the documentary, "Pensions: The Broken Promise." Lawmakers held a series of public hearings that led to ERISA, or the Employee Retirement Income Security Act of 1974. The law was intended to hold employers' feet to the fire and make them fulfill their pension promises. The recession of the 1970s was in full swing, however, and the result was that most large companies simply stopped offering pensions. It wasn't long before defined benefit pension plans were out, and something new was in — defined contribution plans. In other words, you were building your own pension by contributing part of your paycheck to something called a 401(k), a retirement plan that sounded oddly like a vitamin pill. In case you're wondering, the name derives from subsection 401(k) in the Internal Revenue Code. Why was the IRS involved? Because contributions to the plan could be made with pre-taxed dollars and allowed to grow tax free.

All this brought about a seismic shift in the retirement landscape. Now, the responsibility for building and maintaining a retirement nest egg fell squarely on the shoulders of employees, not employers. The employer could match your contribution up to a point, and get a tax break from Uncle Sam, and many did and still do. But employers take no responsibility for the investment outcomes. If it goes south, that's all on the employee. What if the employee is not well acquainted with the intricacies of investing?

What if he or she takes on too much risk when deciding how contributions are invested? That happened to a lot of workers in the major market corrections of 2000 and 2008. It was a case of "too bad, so sad" as far as the employer was concerned.

The Case of Bill

One case that illustrates the point is that of Bill, who was a top producer of an insurance sales organization in the 1990s. Once each year, the company brought in a representative of Fidelity, the custodian who managed the retirement accounts, to discuss with each employee how they wished to have their accounts invested. They gave Bill and other employees four choices:

- **A – Ultra conservative and safe**. Emphasis on money market funds.
- **B – Somewhat conservative.** Mutual funds featuring a mixture of large cap and small cap stock.
- **C – Somewhat risky.** Mutual funds featuring mostly growth stocks, with international stocks thrown in for balance.
- **D – Very risky**. All growth stocks, featuring mutual funds mainly based in the tech sector.

Bill was impulsive. When he heard the word "growth," that's all he needed to hear. He instructed the custodian representative to put all of his contributions in the "growth" option. During the middle 90s, things were great for Bill's 401(k). At the top of each of his quarterly statements was a pie chart showing how his contributions were invested. While other employees had a pie chart with sections, Bill's pie chart looked like a spot. With the tech sector of the economy on fire, it was remarkable how fast Bill's account was growing. Bill would even boast about this at sales meetings with his fellow employees.

Maybe you see where this is going. When the tech bubble burst in 2000, Bill's bubble burst as well, and his account lost years of growth and part of the principal he had invested. He was devastated. He complained to his boss, and to the account's custodian, but received little consolation. He had made the decision.

Careful With That Pension!

If you happen to be one of the fortunate few who has a pension, they are a source of guaranteed income, true, but… well, play along with me for a moment.

Walter has a pension. Let's say it's $5,000 per month. He receives Social Security benefits of $2,000 per month. His wife, Carolyn, gets $1,000 per month in Social Security. That is a total income of $8,000 per month, right?

When Walt retired, he decided that he wanted to put survivor benefits for his wife on 50 percent of his pension. If he were to pass away, she would receive $2,500 monthly. She would also get his Social Security, but she would lose hers.

You see where this is going, don't you? The $8,000 monthly income just dropped to $4,500. You would be surprised at how many couples I come across who make that mistake. All because they don't communicate about the financial aspects of their lives. Couples need to have this kind of dialogue with each other:

"Honey you are irreplaceable. But if you were to die, how much money would it leave me with?" That may be a bit pointed, and maybe not the most romantic of conversations for date night, but you need to know these things, folks. Here's the thing. If we can know it now, we can plan. That way, if it happens, it's not an issue. That is true love. Whether you are married or not, ask yourself if you want a "guaranteed" income or a "maybe" income.

The Four Percent Rule — R.I.P.

The bottom line is this — any income plan based solely on the performance of the stock market is a "maybe" income plan. Anyone who tells you different is either (taking the high road) unqualified to discuss the matter, or (putting it bluntly) outright shining you on.

The so-called "Four Percent Rule" died some time ago, but some financial advisors refuse to acknowledge that the formula on which it was based no longer works in the 21st century. The Four Percent Rule, or Four Percent Withdrawal Rule, as some call it, became popular in the 1990s. The essence of the "rule" was that a retired person could safely withdraw 4 percent from his or her brokerage account each year for 30 years and never run out of money. It was the brainchild of William P. Bengen, a California-based financial planner, who crunched the numbers and came up with the formula. He plugged in several combinations of (a) rates of withdrawal, (b) allocation of assets and (c) duration of retirement before coming up with the magic number — 4.5 percent. Using decades of historical data, he maintained that if a portfolio was properly balanced — 60 percent stocks and 40 percent bonds — and tweaked periodically, it could produce income for 30 years and even withstand inflation of 4 percent.

For easy math, say you accumulated $1 million and parked it with a stockbroker. According to the Four Percent Rule, you could live on $40,000 per year, even adding slightly to it each year for inflation, and go for 30 years, or until the end of your life, whichever came first, and not run out of money. That was the theory, anyway.

Stockbrokers were all over it. It soon became the "Holy Grail" of market-based income planning for retirement. Was there anything wrong with Bengen's research? Not really. He was a pretty smart guy — a graduate of Massachusetts Institute of Technology. Before becoming a financial planner, he successfully managed a soft-drink bottling company. The problem was that he was basing his conclusions on data that did not include the decade of the 2000s and beyond.

Many financial publications in recent years have given the "rule" its last rites and proclaimed it officially dead. One such article, entitled "Say Goodbye to the 4% Rule," written by Kelly Greene, appeared in the March 1, 2013 issue of the Wall Street Journal. Here is a paragraph:

> "If you had retired Jan. 1, 2000, with an initial 4% withdrawal rate and a portfolio of 55% stocks and 45% bonds rebalanced each month, with the first year's withdrawal amount increased by 3% a year for inflation, your portfolio would have fallen by a third through 2010, according to investment firm T. Rowe Price Group. And you would be left with only a 29% chance of making it through three decades, the firm estimates."

With a rapidly changing and volatile economic landscape, investing strategies have an expiration date. The Four Percent Rule was touted as "practically guaranteed," but it just did not stand the test of time. It turned out to be a "definite maybe."

Another article, entitled "Forget the 4% Withdrawal Rule," published by *MONEY* magazine in 2014, quoted Wade Pfau, professor of retirement income at The American College. He lowered the 4 percent withdrawal projection down to 2.22 percent. Translation: If you had $1 million in your brokerage account, you could withdraw just over $20,000 per year for 30 years. I'm not sure, but I think that is bordering on poverty level.

Other headlines and excerpts that spelled the end for the "Four Percent Rule" were:

- **4% Rule for Retirement Withdrawals Is Golden No More** ~ *New York Times, 2013.* "Many financial advisers are rejecting the 4 percent rule as out of touch with present realities."
- **How Much to Withdraw from Retirement Savings** ~ Forbes magazine, 2013. "When the 4% rule emerged, investment portfolios were earning about 8% annually. Today, they're generally in the 3 to 4% range."
- **Retirees May Need to Rethink 4% Rule** ~ AARP, 2013. "... new research by Morningstar Investment Management suggests that relying on that 4 percent rule of thumb today

is risky, thanks to a market in which bond yields and dividends have hovered at record lows for years."

Projections vs. Guarantees

If you are discussing a retirement income plan and hear words like: "projection, estimated, approximately, probably or probability," you have a "maybe income" to look forward to. If you want a guaranteed income, listen for words like: "guaranteed, lifetime, absolutely and positively." It is about as simple as that.

Is there such a thing as guaranteed income in today's topsy-turvy investing world? Can you have guarantees with growth?

As they used to say in the old days of radio: "Stay tuned. Don't touch that dial!"

CHAPTER FIVE

Fees - The Devil Is in the Details

"Nothing in fine print is ever good news." ~ Andy Rooney

I don't know about you, but I detest fine print. It's in everything from labels on food to your phone bill. I get more concerned the smaller the print gets. It is usually the means by which the provider of the information attempts to satisfy some law that requires them to disclose information, but they don't really want you to pay attention. Why do I get the feeling they are trying to slip something by you? Is it because they are?

Banks like to slip in fees. Maintenance fees, transaction fees, ATM fees. I'm not saying they are altogether hidden, but you will never see a sign near a bank counter that reads, "We Charge More Fees."

Do you understand your phone bill? Me neither. Service fees, roaming charges, taxes, government surcharges. Do you just shut your eyes and pay it? Me too. And just try to have an amicable separation from your cellphone carrier. They will remind you that you have another think coming because you signed an agreement you probably didn't read wherein you promised to stay together for at least two years. What do you call that? "Phonimony?"

Consumer Reports tells us even our friendly local supermarket cannot be trusted to be straight with us. To hike prices without us suspecting it, big food producers have started shrinking the containers and charging the same amount, hoping we won't notice. According to a 2011 article in *Consumer Reports,* one example is a carton of ice cream that used to contain 16 ounces, but now contains only 14 ounces, and costs the same. These companies must think they are dealing with a bunch of naïve shoppers who don't pay attention! And they would be right.

Nontransparency in Investments

I'll bet you a Moon Pie and an RC Cola that most of you who own mutual funds and variable annuities don't realize how much you pay in fees and hidden charges. (If you are under the age of 40, or live above the Mason-Dixon line, see me or my son, Drew, personally for an explanation of the colloquialism.)

I'm not just talking about the advisor fee; I'm talking about fees inside of the investment. Today's investment landscape is full of hidden fees and unexpected and unexplained charges. The worst offenders are mutual funds, but they are certainly not alone.

Barron's, a respected financial magazine, ran an article in its issue of March 2, 2013, entitled, "The High Cost of Doing Business" that exposed a deception that has been going on for years (and is still going on). Aiming her guns primarily at mutual funds, writer Beverly Goodman cited the research of Roger Edelen, a finance professor at University of California, which reveals the "invisible costs that eat away at returns." Among these, the worst seem to be "trading costs," or, as they are also called, "transaction costs."

Goodman explains:

"Transaction or trading costs include the commissions paid, the bid-ask spread on each transaction, and the price, or market, impact of funds buying or selling big blocks of shares. (When a fund buys or sells a substantial amount of a company's stock, it can "move the market," causing the share price to rise or fall, thereby putting it in the unfortunate position of continuing to buy while the price is rising, or selling as the price is falling.)"

The thing is, investors pay no attention to this when the funds are performing well. They consider it, as the title of the article suggests, a "cost of doing business." It's only when the funds lose money that these hidden fees show up like sharp rocks at low tide. Goodman estimates the average mutual fund investor pays 1.44 percent annually in trading costs, *whether or not you are receiving positive returns!*

Commissions are disclosed in the mutual fund's prospectus, but that, too, is misleading, according to Goodman.

"A cynic would say the industry loves that," Edelen says. "They can make the stated commissions arbitrarily low, but Wall Street finds a way to get paid."

With mutual funds, some of the fees are in the prospectus. Have you ever sat down with a cup of coffee, slipped on your reading glasses and settled down in your easy chair and spent a relaxing evening reading a mutual fund prospectus? Of course not. We treat them like the "Terms and Conditions" document we agree to before activating an app on our smartphones. Which is to say, we close our eyes and just hit the "I Agree" button. The average investor just shrugs and signs because the language is too difficult to comprehend. Fund firms don't seem willing to make the language any less confusing. Why is that? Would the mutual fund companies prefer we remain ignorant and unaware?

The article, "The Investment Fees You Don't Realize You're Paying," which appeared in the Dec. 15, 2014 issue of U.S. News and World Report, had this to say: "Rebalance IRA asked 1,165 baby boomers between ages 50 and 68, all with full-time jobs, how much they were paying in investment fees. Forty-six percent believed they paid nothing, and 19 percent were under the impression that their fees totaled less than 0.5 percent. In fact, according to data cited by Rebalance IRA, employees have retirement account expense deductions averaging 1.5 percent per year."

The article's author, Kate Stalter, offers the following suggestions (with which I heartily agree) to avoid hidden investment fees:[12]

Have an investment strategy — Instead of just investing for investing's sake, identify your goals and risk tolerance. Once you establish a strategy, stick with it and stay disciplined.

Consider the type of investment carefully — Some accounts are taxable and some are not. Know the difference. A taxable account with a high level of trading will cost you more.

Know how your financial advisor is paid — Is the advisor a traditional broker who is paid a commission every time a trade is made? Or is he or she a Registered Investment Advisor who receives a percentage of assets under management or a flat fee?

Read and understand your statement — She uses the example of one financial advisor who reportedly broke out the fees on a portfolio quarterly. The investor was paying 0.37 percent per quarter, which totals out to 1.5 per year. You had to do the math and multiply times four to get the true picture.

Understand mutual fund fee structures — Learn the difference between Class A, B, C, R and I. Some have front-end loads deducted from the initial investment. Look for 12b-1 fees. Those are internal expenses and they are built into most mutual funds. Check out the

---

[12] Kate Stalter. U.S. News & World Report Money. Dec. 15, 2014. "The Investment Fees You Don't Realize You're Paying." http://money.usnews.com/money/personal-finance/mutual-funds/articles/2014/12/15/the-investment-fees-you-dont-realize-youre-paying.

internal expense ratio. Naturally, the lower the cost, the more of your returns you get to keep if the fund does well.

Let's say you have a half-million dollars in a mutual fund portfolio and you are paying 2 percent in fees. Two percent of $500,000 is $10,000. That's how much you are paying per year for that investment. Has the fund's performance in the last 10 years or so warranted that kind of fee? It's doubtful. Get an objective analysis from an unbiased advisor you trust if you think any of this applies to you. Also remember this: The mutual fund industry advertises performance but talks little about cost. But high costs erode good performance.

Brokerage Account Fees

It should come as no surprise to us that stockbrokers and brokerage firms charge commissions. They are in competition with other stockbrokers and other brokerage firms. That is why they publish commission comparison tables. Have you ever picked one of these advertisements up and tried to decipher it? The ones I have seen appear to be purposely incomprehensible. You tend to get lost in the asterisks and fine print. Each company tries to make you think that it charges less in commissions by "creative" advertising. For example, one broker will post $8 per trade while another claims $15 per trade. Naturally, you are led to believe that the $8 company is cheaper. The fine print may reveal a different story. You may pay hefty additional charges for talking to a living, breathing human about your investment. You may pay an "inactivity fee" if you leave the account idle. Some brokerage firms charge you to deposit money into the account.

You don't notice the fees and charges if the market is on a roll, but the sleight-of-hand is amplified when the account loses money.

SEC Cautions Investors

If you visit the United States Securities and Exchange Commission's website, www.sec.gov, you will find the following paragraphs under the heading "Calculating Mutual Fund Fees and Expenses":[13]

"Fees and expenses are an important consideration in selecting a mutual fund because **these charges lower your returns.** Many investors find it helpful to compare the fees and expenses of different mutual funds before they invest...

"...A mutual fund's fees and expenses may be more important than you realize. Advertisements, rankings, and ratings often emphasize how well a fund has performed in the past. But studies show that the future is often different. This year's "number one" fund can easily become next year's below average fund."

---

[13] U.S. Securities and Exchange Commission. Aug. 10, 2010. "Calculating Mutual Fund Fees and Expenses." http://www.sec.gov/investor/tools/mfcc/mfcc-int.htm.

CHAPTER SIX

Long-Term Care - The Elephant in the Living Room

"Be nice to your children. After all, they are going to choose your nursing home." ~ Steven Wright

Long-term care is an eventuality we don't like to think about, let alone discuss at a family dinner. It's like the proverbial "elephant in the living room" — a very large issue that all are aware of but would rather not acknowledge is there.

Please don't shoot the messenger, but I need to bring it up in this book because no retirement planning is effective unless we face facts. Have you looked at the statistics lately of how likely it is that you will eventually be confined to a nursing home, or end up in an assisted living facility? The probability is expressed in different ways by various research groups.

"About 70 percent of people now age 65 and older will need some period of extended care during the remainder of their life," claims U.S. News and World Report.[14]

Morningstar, an investment research group based in Chicago, Illinois, says that if you live to be age 65, there is a 40 percent chance you will enter a nursing home at some point in your lifetime.[15]

Dr. Muriel Gillick, in her 2007 book, "The Denial of Aging," says:

"The latest prediction is that if you are just now turning 65, you have nearly a 50 percent chance of spending some time in a nursing home before you die."

Regardless, the probability of needing long-term care is high enough to motivate millions of Americans to pay high premiums in exchange for the peace of mind of knowing that (a) they won't be financially wiped out, (b) end up being a burden on their loved ones or (c) become a ward of the state and forced to opt for sub-standard care.

The Cost of Long-Term Care

What does long-term care cost in the area where you plan to live out your retirement? It depends. Costs vary widely from one place to another. For example, Genworth Insurance, a leading provider of long-term care coverage, lists New York State as one of the most expensive — around $132,000 for a semi-private room in a nursing home. Louisiana is one of the least expensive states. There, it will cost you an average of around $56,000 for the same care. In Florida,

---

[14] Philip Moeller. U.S. News & World Report Money. June 15, 2012. "How Nursing Home Stays Ravage Finances." http://money.usnews.com/money/blogs/the-best-life/2012/06/15/how-nursing-home-stays-ravage-finances.

[15] Christine Benz. Morningstar. Aug. 9, 2012. "40 Must-Know Statistics About Long-Term Care." http://news.morningstar.com/articlenet/article.aspx?id=564139.

where my son, Drew, and I work and live, a semi-private room averages $87,600 per year.[16]

Private rooms in nursing homes cost more, of course. You will also pay considerably less for adult day care and assisted living facilities. But here's the bottom line: Long-term care costs can quickly wipe out a retirement nest egg it may have taken you decades to accumulate. We encourage clients to do their own due diligence (we are happy to help, of course).

Money is not the only consideration. If you are to the point where the use of one of these facilities seems likely for you, you will have plenty of places from which to choose. Explore your options. According to the Florida Health Care Association, there are 681 nursing homes in the state.[17]

Nowadays, there are also continuing care retirement centers, active adult communities and retirement communities galore, especially in Florida. The culture varies widely from one facility to another. Why not visit facilities that are under consideration? Speak personally with the activities director. You want to find out which ones offer the best atmosphere and quality of life. It is perfectly alright (even recommended) to casually interview residents. Walk the halls. Check out the living quarters. Inspect the rehabilitation and exercise programs. Eat in the dining rooms. Look at the fitness rooms. It may be important to you that they have a spiritual culture there. Ask about it. My advice is to learn all you can about the facility that best fits your needs and make your preference known to your loved ones. That prevents someone else from making decisions for you, and keeps you from having to make a decision

---

[16] Genworth. April 2015. "Genworth 2015 Cost of Care Survey." https://www.genworth.com/corporate/about-genworth/industry-expertise/cost-of-care.html.

[17] Florida Health Care Association. "Fact About Long Term Care in Florida." http://www.fhca.org/media_center/long_term_health_care_facts.

under pressure. If you never need to live there, then the information can stay in your files.

The LTC Insurance Dilemma

Sam and his wife, Janet, both age 60, were considering purchasing a long-term care (LTC) insurance policy to cover both of them. They were shocked when they discovered it would cost them more than $6,500 per year for a policy that would pay them $250 per day in a nursing home for three years. They were also surprised to learn:

- Before they could buy the policy, they would have to prove they were healthy enough to qualify.
- Premiums could go up at some point in the future, and they would have no choice but to pay the higher premiums or lose the coverage.
- If they never need the coverage, the policy would not refund any portion of the premiums, and no cash value would accrue.

If Sam and Janet wait until they are age 65 to purchase LTC insurance, it will cost them nearly $8,700 per year for the two of them.[18] Meanwhile, the cost of long-term care keeps increasing 4–5 percent per year.[19]

Use It or Lose It

Susan purchased a similar LTC policy at age 54. She pays around $200 per month, or $2,400 annually for the coverage. She anticipated that when she retired, she would have her Social Security income, a small pension and a few investments to use to pay her bills, including the LTC premiums. It fit within her budget, but barely.

---

[18] The Federal Long Term Care Insurance Program. https://www.ltcfeds.com/ltcWeb/do/assessing_your_needs/ratecalcOut.

[19] Genworth. April 2015. "Genworth 2015 Cost of Care Survey." https://www.genworth.com/dam/Americas/US/PDFs/Consumer/corporate/130568_040115_gnw.pdf.

Her reasoning was simple — if she had to go to a nursing facility, she could be wiped out financially without insurance. She hated the thought of becoming a burden on her daughter. And she knew her care options would be limited if she were to deplete her savings and be forced to rely on Medicaid. So buying the insurance seemed the only practical thing to do.

Thirteen years later, when Susan is 67 and retired, she gets a letter from the insurance carrier. Her $200 monthly premium is going up. The letter explains that the insurance company has shown proof to the government that they are losing money on the group of enrollees of which Susan is a part. Her new premium will be $370 per month. This hits her hard. She can't afford to drop the policy and lose all the money she has paid into it, and she can't afford the new premiums. She can reduce the benefits by lengthening her elimination period (the amount of time before her benefits start to pay out), or she can reduce the period of coverage. Tough decision.

While that is a composite based on a hypothetical case, it is a very real scenario. Insurance carriers are feeling the pinch from steadily rising long-term care costs and the aging population of enrollees. That's why rates are going up, and some carriers are even leaving the market.[20]

Not Covered by Medicare

"Hey, doesn't Medicare cover long-term care?"

No. If you want to see that in print, just consult the 2016 edition of "Medicare and You," the official U.S. government Medicare handbook. Here's a quote:

---

[20] Kathleen Kingsbury. Reuters, as appearing in the Chicago Tribune. April 13, 2012. "Long-term care dilemma." http://articles.chicagotribune.com/2012-04-13/business/sc-cons-0412-save-long-term-care-20120413_1_long-term-care-insurance-individual-policies-home-care.

"Long-term care includes non-medical care for people who have a chronic illness or disability. This includes non-skilled personal care assistance, like help with everyday activities, including dressing, bathing, and using the bathroom. *Medicare and most health insurance plans, including Medicare Supplement Insurance (Medigap) policies, don't pay for this type of care, sometimes called "custodial care."* Long-term care can be provided at home, in the community, in an assisted living facility, or in a nursing home. It's important to start planning for long-term care now to maintain your independence and to make sure you get the care you may need, in the setting you want, in the future." (The italics are ours.)

What About Medicaid?

Medicaid was created in 1965 during the Great Society initiatives of President Lyndon B. Johnson, and was intended to pay for health care for the poor. As things have worked out, however, it has become a benefit for lots of middle-class Americans who exhaust their savings and have no choice but to rely on the government dole.

Over the years, I have known several individuals who went from property-owning, tax-paying citizens to folks who had to depend on the state to pay for their care after their health failed them. According to AARP, Medicaid has become the "primary payer for more than 60 percent of long-stay nursing home residents," even though it is supposed to be a "program of last resort." The AARP Public Policy Institute contends that average Americans are forced to turn to Medicaid because of the high cost of long-term support and services. Millions of Americans each year dispose of their assets in order to fit the poverty guidelines and qualify for Medicaid. It's not illegal. In fact, the government knows it goes on and has instituted what they call a "five-year lookback" policy to make it difficult for senior citizens to use loopholes like giving money to their children when they learn they must receive long-term care. They can still do that, but they have to do it five years before they need the care.[21]

Some who are not aware of the five-year lookback policy learn the hard way that the rules are strictly enforced. Medicaid is a federally funded program, but it is administered by the state. If an examiner audits a recipient of Medicaid-funded LTC and discovers an infraction, eligibility can be withdrawn.

The term "spend down" is associated with the process of disposing of assets to qualify for Medicaid. Certain items, such as burial plots and pre-paid funeral arrangements are on the list of authorized expenses when an individual is trying to "spend down" their assets in order to qualify for Medicaid. Giving money to children at any point in the five-year look back is a violation of the rules.[22]

Qualifying for Medicaid is not the optimal solution to the long-term care dilemma. It puts you at the mercy of the state, and the quality of care is often sub-par.[23]

New Solutions

Long-term care insurance is not that old. It first came on the scene in the 1970s. Back then, it was affordable for consumers and profitable for insurance companies. As time passed, however, higher health care costs led to higher premiums and fewer enrollees. Claim loss was higher and patients were living longer. Some

[21] Donald Redfoot and Wendy Fox-Grage. AARP Public Policy Institute. "Medicaid: A Program of Last Resort for People Who Need Long-Term Services and Supports." INSIGHT on the Issues 81. May, 2013.

[22] Elder Law Answers. Aug. 27, 2013. "How to Deal With Medicaid's Five-Year Look-Back Period." http://www.elderlawanswers.com/how-to-deal-with-medicaids-five-year-look-back-period-12438.

[23] Medicaid.gov. "Medicaid and CHIP Program Information." 2014. https://www.medicaid.gov/medicaid-chip-program-information/medicaid-and-chip-program-information.html.

of the larger carriers threw in the towel — Prudential Financial in 2012 and MetLife in 2010. Other carriers were forced to raise their premiums. Meanwhile, the need for long-term care coverage is steadily increasing. Ed Beeson of the Newark, New Jersey Star-Ledger, writes: "Despite the challenges facing the market, experts say the need for long-term care coverage won't go away. The research and consulting firm LIMRA estimates that by 2020 there will be about 12 million Americans who are 65 and older in need of a long-term care policy."[24]

In the 1990s, with sales of traditional long-term care insurance losing market share, a few big insurance companies called in their actuaries and product design people and asked them to come up with a fresh approach. The result was the introduction of hybrid insurance products that combined LTC coverage with life insurance and annuities. Called "combos" (combination products) by insurance industry insiders, they have been attracting more and more attention from retiring baby boomers in recent years.

Life insurance combos allow the insured to accelerate the death benefit should they become chronically or terminally ill. In other words, you don't have to die for the policy to pay. Policyholders have the option of using a percentage of the death benefit to pay for long-term care if they qualify. To collect on the "living benefits" of these policies, the insured must be unable to perform at least two of six "activities of daily living" (ADLs): eating, dressing, toileting, walking, bathing and continence. If the long-term care cost turns out to be less than the death benefit, and the insured dies, the beneficiary of the policy gets whatever is left over. That's just a thumbnail sketch of how these policies work, but you get the idea. That

---

[24] Ed Beeson. The Star-Ledger. March 25, 2012. "Long-term care insurance market shrinking as Prudential, others pull back." http://www.nj.com/news/index.ssf/2012/03/insurers_including_njs_prudent.html.

way, the "use it or lose it" aspect of traditional LTC insurance is eliminated.

Annuity combos allow you to either retire on the money you have deposited into an annuity or use it to defray long-term care costs. Plans vary, but an example would be as follows: You are 60 years old. You deposit $50,000 into an LTC annuity. If you need the care, you may use up to three times the amount you deposited ($150,000) for that care over a specified period. If you do not need the care — if you never need the services of a nursing home or assisted living facility, for example — your money wasn't wasted. It grew at interest (in most cases) and passed on to heirs (in most cases) at your death.

"Facing facts is part of effective planning."

Just a word of caution: These products are still relatively new. Check with a qualified and fully licensed financial advisor and know all your options before purchasing one.

A Change of Heart

Many years ago, a lady in her early 80s came in for counseling. She was healthy and alert, but she had been thinking about the possibility of her needing long-term care at some point in the future. She was charmingly candid about her situation.

"Well, David, I am concerned," she began. "I have one son. He lives three states away in the Carolinas. If something happened to me today, I don't want him to have to worry about taking care of me."

We began discussing solutions. The average cost of long-term care back then was around $40,000 per year. She had enough money to cover the first year of such care. But not for two or three years.

We looked at a long-term care policy that would provide $150,000 in coverage for her over a three-year period. Because of her age, the premiums were rather expensive, but she made it clear this was what she wanted. We completed the application, and I told her I would submit it for her the next day.

That night, I received a phone call from her son. He was angry and upset.

"My mom does not need this insurance policy," he said. "I am going to take care of her. I am driving down there to see her this weekend, and I want to meet with you and her."

The three of us met the following week, and the son was much calmer in person than he had been on the phone. I assured him I had nothing but his and his mother's best interests at heart. He re-iterated his position that his mother did not need long term care protection, and that he would take care of her.

I looked at the woman and said, "Ma'am, that is fantastic. What your son is saying is that if something happens and you get to where you can't perform two of the six activities of daily living, he is going to move you to his house in the Carolinas and take care of you."

The son, waving his hands in the no-no-no gesture, said "That's not what I said. I just said I am going to take care of her."

"Oh, I am confused," I said. "The long-term care policy carries $150,000 in benefits. So what you're really saying is that you've set aside $150,000 of your own money, and you are going to use it to take care of her, right?"

"No," he said. "I didn't say that at all!"

Then, turning to the mother, I said, "Then I suppose what your son is really saying to you is that if you get to the point where you can't take care of yourself, he is going to come feed you, dress you, bathe you and, in general, take care of you 24-7."

The son was quiet for a moment, and then said, "Mom, I sure hope that insurance policy gets approved."

As I said at the beginning of this chapter, long-term care is one of those emotional issues that some would prefer not to discuss. It's understandable (and regrettable). We all tend to think with our hearts and not our heads when our emotions are involved. When your kids say, "Don't worry, I will take care of you," that is an admirable sentiment, but it is not a plan.

Facing facts is part of effective planning. Abraham Lincoln was once asked: "How many legs does a dog have if you call the tail a leg?" After stroking his beard for a moment, he gave the answer: "Four. Calling the tail a leg doesn't make it a leg."

Pretending the elephant is not in the room doesn't make it not there. Let someone like Drew or me help you plan for long-term care contingencies. It is not as complicated, nor is it as expensive, as you may think.

CHAPTER SEVEN

Having a Purpose for Your Money

"When you dance, your purpose is not to get to a certain place on the floor. It's to enjoy each step along the way." ~ Wayne Dyer

When we ask prospective clients to tell us how they would define the *purpose* of their money, some have an answer clearly in mind. Without hesitating, they can give us concise and thorough details.

"I want to retire at age 65, with an income of $70,000 per year. I would also like to spend a year touring Europe and then the Holy Land."

"We would like to retire three years from now, sell the business, sell the house and live at the beach."

"We want to make sure our grandchildren get a university education."

Some, however, do not have a ready answer. That does not necessarily mean they have no purpose for their wealth. It could just be they find it difficult to put their mental pictures into words. Some people are better than others at visualizing the future.

But one surprising thing is this: with most people, their **investments** don't line up with their stated **purpose.** Again, this is not necessarily a poor reflection on them. They probably just failed to receive the financial education they needed from a fiduciary (there's that word again... please stay tuned, we will discuss it later in this book) professional who was willing to help them put their money to work in the most effective possible way to achieve their individual life goals.

When people sit down with me to discuss the **purpose** of their money and start talking about their grandchildren, or where they want to live or travel, I know we are off to a good start.

But quite often, when I ask the "purpose" question, the responses I hear reveal a disconnect. The conversation may go something like this:

Me: "I see you have $200,000 invested in ABC mutual funds. Why?"

Them: "I don't know."

Me: "And it looks like you have $50,000 in three variable annuities. Do you know why you made that decision?"

Them: "No, not really."

Me: "Do you remember even making that decision?"

Them: "No, not really."

Health-Wealth Comparison

It's a case of their **why** not matching their **what, where** and **how much.**

And some of these people are highly educated, intelligent folks. It's hard to imagine them being that uninformed about their wealth. Can you imagine someone having a conversation like this with their doctor?

Doctor: "I see you are taking 50 milligrams of Hydromexadry-othelene three times a day. Why?"

Patient: "I don't know."

Doctor: "You are also taking pills to reduce cholesterol. Do you have high cholesterol?"

Patient: "I don't know."

Being that out of touch with your health can harm you *physically.* Being out of touch with your wealth can harm you *fiscally.*

Bottom line: First, arrive at your WHY. Then adjust your WHAT, WHERE and HOW MUCH to match.

Money Without Purpose

When you stop and think about it, money without purpose amounts to just so many numbers. Numbers on currency, numbers on a bank statement, maybe numbers beside a stock market ticker symbol or on a computer screen.

Let's get philosophical for just a moment. Everything in life breaks down into one of two categories: concrete and abstract. Numbers are abstracts. They are merely symbols. But when you get your paycheck, do the numbers matter? You bet they do! Zeros are numbers. Would it bother you to have some of those zeroes removed from the end of that number on your paycheck? Absolutely! The more zeroes, the better!

That's another thing. Numbers never end. How many zeroes can you add to a number? As many as you wish. But you get to a point where your comprehension dims and the number becomes pointless. Take, for example, the distance from Earth to Pluto, the most distant planet in our solar system. Saying Pluto is 4 billion miles from Earth doesn't really convey much. You have to put it terms we can understand, like speed and travel time. NASA did that for us on Jan. 19, 2006 when they launched a piano-sized space vehicle named New Horizons. Its mission was to take close-up photographs of

Pluto. Even though it zipped through space at 31,000 miles per hour (18 times faster than a rifle bullet), it still took more than 9 years to get there. Images began to appear back on Earth on July 14, 2015.[25]

Is it difficult for you to wrap your mind around that kind of speed, and that kind of distance? Yeah. Me too. All we can do is gasp in awe at the pictures and marvel at the technology that produced them.

If New Horizons had just been zipping aimlessly through the universe, it would have been a waste of time and resources. But its purpose was to get close enough to what had previously been a blurry dot in the black sky to let us see the face of our celestial neighbor. Just like that spacecraft, money is nothing without *purpose.*

It cost the U.S. taxpayers $700 million, by the way, to make that happen. Was it worth it? It depends on whom you ask. When the pictures appeared on TV, people were excited to see them. Now we know that ice mountains 15,000 feet high exist on Pluto. But is that knowledge worth $700 million? You see, we are back where we started, aren't we? What's money anyway? It represents only the *purpose* we give it. What can you do with $700 million? You could:

- Pay the annual salaries for around 12,000 school teachers.[26]
- Install 200 wind turbines to provide power for 65,000 homes.[27]
- Pay for a 100-mile stretch of interstate highway,[28] or

---

[25] Nola Taylor Redd. Space.com. Feb. 20, 2016. "How Far Away is Pluto?" http://www.space.com/18566-pluto-distance.html.

[26] National Center for Education Statistics. Digest of Education Statistics. 2013. "Estimated average annual salary of teachers in public elementary and secondary schools, by state." https://nces.ed.gov/programs/digest/d13/tables/dt13_211.60.asp.

[27] National Wind Watch. "FAQ-Output." https://www.wind-watch.org/faq-output.php.

[28] American Road & Transportation Builders Association. 2016. "Transportation FAQs." http://www.artba.org/about/transportation-faqs/.

- Solve the celestial mysteries of a distant planet.

It all comes down to purpose and priorities, folks.

Investing With a Purpose

When I first began helping people plan their financial futures in 1998, it occurred to me that most people needed two things: an ultimate goal and education on how to achieve it.

Too many people these days invest with no ultimate purpose in mind. To use a boating metaphor, they have plenty of sail but not enough rudder. In an actual boat, without a rudder you would be pushed around by the waves and could end up way off course in dangerous waters. The winds of the stock market are fickle and unpredictable. Investors without a plan are subject to unnecessary taxation and market volatility. Without a clear purpose in view, our financial vision can become blurred. As Yogi Berra put it, "Be careful if you don't know where you're going. You might not get there."

A purpose-driven financial plan addresses your individual values and aspirations. The idea is not just to amass as much wealth as possible, but to ensure a confident and fulfilling life for you and your family.

Different Strokes/Different Folks

No two people are alike.

What about identical twins? Nope, not even identical twins. They have the same DNA, but different fingerprints. No matter how similar two individuals may be — same age, same job, same salary, same size family, same investments and same net worth — they will still need different financial plans. Why? Because they will have different values, goals, dreams, hopes, desires and ambitions. It only stands to reason, then, that no two financial plans will be identical.

Not Ready for Retirement

It troubles me when I read that Americans aren't saving as much money as they used to. According to statistics reported by the Employee Benefit Research Institute in "The 2015 Retirement Confidence Survey," 28 percent of Americans have savings of less than $1,000. Fifty-seven percent have savings of less than $25,000.[29]

To make matters worse, the statistics on personal debt in America are alarming. In 2015, outstanding credit card debt in the U.S. was more than $712 billion and student loan debt was a staggering $1.21 trillion! Yep. There is more student loan debt on the books now than credit card debt. The cost of personal debt in the U.S. is 9 percent of the average household income, an average of $6,658 per year in *interest alone.*[30]

I was also a bit disturbed to see the following statistic in the 2015 "Social Security Administration Basic Facts" report:[31]

- Among elderly Social Security beneficiaries, 22% of married couples and about 47% of unmarried persons rely on Social Security for 90% or more of their income. That's flirting with the poverty line.

The Savings Shortfall

One of the most comprehensive reports I have ever read on the state of retirement in the United States appeared in the 2015

---

[29] Ruth Helman (Greenwald & Associates), Craig Copeland and Jack VanDerhei. Employee Benefit Research Institute. April 2015. "The 2015 Retirement Confidence Survey: Having a Retirement Savings Plan a Key Factor in Americans' Retirement Confidence." https://www.ebri.org/publications/ib/index.cfm?fa=ibDisp&content_id=5513.

[30] Erin El Issa. NerdWallet. 2015. "2015 American Household Credit Card Debt Study. https://www.nerdwallet.com/blog/credit-card-data/average-credit-card-debt-household/.

[31] Social Security Administration. Oct. 13, 2015. "Social Security Basic Facts." https://www.ssa.gov/news/press/basicfact.html.

Accounting Degree Review, a newsletter for finance and accounting students. The report, entitled "The Crisis in Pensions and Retirement Plans," put forth the following information:[32]

- Over the next 40 years, people over 65 will account for 20% of the U.S. population.
- By 2050, people over 85 will be as large a percentage of the population (4.6%) as people over 65 were in 1930.
- 50% of all American workers have less than $2,000 saved for retirement.
- 36% of Americans don't contribute anything to retirement savings.

Fears About Social Security

- 6 out of every 10 nonretirees in the United States believe the Social Security system will not be able to pay benefits to them when they retire.
- 35% of Americans over 65 rely almost entirely on Social Security payments.
- 56% of current retirees believe the government will cut their Social Security benefits.
- In 1950, each retiree's Social Security benefit was paid by 16 U.S. workers.
- In 2010, each retiree's Social Security benefit was paid by approximately 3.3 U.S. workers
- By 2025, there will be 2 workers for every 1 retiree.

Set Goals, Young People

If I could build what I'm about to say in big block letters the size of the Hollywood sign and paint them fluorescent orange so every

---

[32] Accounting Degree Review. 2015. "The Crisis in Pensions and Retirement Plans." http://www.accounting-degree.org/retirement.

young person would have to pay attention, I would: **SET GOALS!** Give your financial life a direction.

According to a study conducted by Dave Kohl, professor emeritus at Virginia Tech, 80 percent of Americans say they don't have goals. Another 16 percent say they have goals, but they just don't write them down. What you should do, of course, is write your goals down and review them regularly. Only one out of 100 people do that, Kohl said.[33]

There is a definite correlation between setting goals and accumulating wealth. Having something to reach for gives us a sense of anticipation about the future. It fuels our engine of accomplishment. We enjoy living in the present more because we are going somewhere. Just the fact that you *have* goals will cause your lifetime wealth to increase by 20 percent, experts say.

Reasons to Put Goals in Writing:

- Forces you to focus on them. Crystalizes your thinking.
- Makes you accountable. If you take a list to the grocery store or hardware store, you are more likely to get all the items.
- Helps you remember them. If, at the end of the year, you look at your goals and see that you missed achieving one or two, don't worry. You can write them down again for the New Year.
- It's more like a contract.

Goals Need to Be S.M.A.R.T.

If you are like most people, you envision your future — what kind of job you want, what kind of car you want to drive, what kind of house you want to live in. But obtaining those things as you

---

[33] Daniel Wong. The Duke Chronicle. April 6, 2011. "Reflections of a compulsive goal-setter." http://www.dukechronicle.com/article/2011/04/reflections-compulsive-goal-setter.

imagine them usually requires dogged determination. For goals to truly motivate us toward the accumulation of wealth, they must be S.M.A.R.T. That is, **specific, measurable, attainable, realistic** and **time-sensitive**. Let's take them one at a time from the perspective of accumulating wealth.[34]

Specific: When you specify the exact thing you wish to accomplish, you have a much greater chance of doing it. For example, "Land a good-paying job" is not specific enough. You need to write: "Earn $50,000 per year by age 23." You could even be more specific. "Earn $50,000 per year in salary as a chemical engineer," or "Earn $50,000 per year by increasing monthly production in my territory to $300,000 in 18 months." Goals like that give you traction. General goals just spin your wheels.

Measurable: For a goal to be meaningful, it must be measurable. A physical fitness goal may be, "I want to run three miles in 20 minutes." Or, "I want to lose 10 pounds in 30 days." A wealth goal will be measurable, as well. I want to accumulate $10,000 in savings in 18 months. This gives us the ability to track our progress. If we wish to accumulate $10,000 in 18 months, we will have to put aside $555.55 per month. When we measure our progress and stay on course, reaching our target dates, we have a sense of accomplishment to encourage us to the finish line.

"Written, specific goals are much more likely to be achieved than vague goals perceived but not penned."

To accumulate wealth, you may want to take other things into account. These measurable savings goals may not seem powerful at

---

[34] Kori Morgan. eHow. "Examples of High School S.M.A.R.T. Goals." http://www.ehow.com/info_12309012_examples-high-school-smart-goals.html.

first. But if you were to start by saving $1,000 initially, then add $600 on a monthly basis with an average yearly interest rate of 10 percent, you will have $1,265,960 in 30 years. That's the power of measurable goals.

Attainable: In the above illustration, becoming a millionaire in 30 years is pretty impressive! But if saving $600 per month turns out to be impossible, it will do you no good to set such a goal. It will only discourage you. Your goal may require some effort and sacrifice, but it must be *reachable, or attainable.* If your goals are too difficult, you won't even try. If your goals are too easy, you won't stretch. The time frame you assign to the goal must be reasonable, too. Telling yourself you want to lose 10 pounds in 10 hours is wishful thinking. Attainable goals allow you to grow in your self-worth when you accomplish them.

Realistic: This is almost the same as attainable, but with a subtle difference. To be realistic, a goal must represent an objective toward which you are both *willing* and *able* to work. No one but you can decide just how high your goal should be. But it should be both high and realistic and represent substantial personal progress when you achieve it.

Time-sensitive: Meaningful goals occupy a time frame. Without a time limit, there is no urgency. "I want to lose 10 pounds one of these days," has no sense of urgency tied to it. "I want to lose 10 pounds by June 1 this year" gives the goal a time limit and makes it real to you. If the goal is reasonable, attainable, realistic, specific and falls within a time frame, you are motivated to work on it by degrees and achieve it. A money goal with the same elements is a powerful tool toward accumulating wealth.

Break Goals Into Sections

When you are setting goals for yourself, break them up into sections. You won't forget them that way, and each section you accomplish is a small victory, the small parts adding up to a whole. Set yearly goals, and then quarterly goals, and finally monthly goals.

If you have a significant other with whom your share your life, it helps to share your goals with them. Post them in a conspicuous place. Mark your achievements on a calendar. Celebrate when you meet them. Make it a family affair. Review your goals periodically and make adjustments if necessary. If you have a savings goal of, say, $100 per month, and you receive a substantial increase in salary, then revisit your goal and adjust it accordingly.

Make decisions in harmony with your goals. Let's say you and your spouse are striving to pay off your automobile loans by the end of the year and to keep on track with your savings goals of $200 per month. You are invited by a group of friends to take an expensive ski vacation. You can take the trip, and you will have many cherished memories, but it will delay paying off your auto loan, and it will derail your savings plan. It's decision time. One thing about money, you can either have the things it will buy, or you can have the money, but you can't have both. Moments like these will test your mettle as a goal setter. Often the sense of fulfillment and satisfaction of reaching a goal will provide the impetus for staying the course and not giving in. On the other hand, if you can sell something you don't need on eBay and work some overtime between now and then, then you can take the trip and stay on track with your goals at the same time.

Goals are magical motivators that enable you to live where you want to live, do the kind of work you want to do, enjoy both your working life and your retirement to a greater degree. They can change you for the better and allow you to become the kind of person you wish to become.

Getting Serious

I believe the reason so few people set goals is they don't "get serious" about things. Whenever I interview highly successful people and ask them how they achieved their success, they will usually tell me about a point in their lives when they just decided to "get serious," about life, about work, about their savings program. Apparently, nothing happens until you "get serious" about it.

It could also be that young people who aren't in the habit of setting goals don't realize how important goals can be. Young people who began setting scholastic achievement goals while in school usually come from families in which goals were emphasized. Their parents probably set goals and discussed them around the dinner table.

Are there classes in high school on goal setting? I haven't heard of them. But there should be. Most of my clients are either retired or on the threshold of retirement, but I do occasionally work with young people, and I find they get downright excited about goal setting once they see the power behind it.

CHAPTER EIGHT

Suitability vs. Fiduciary Advice

"One of the funny things about the stock market is that every time one person buys, another sells, and both think they are astute." ~ William Feather

Over my years as a financial counselor, I have encountered many people who have been "sold" a product, or placed in an investment strategy that was not appropriate for them and not a "custom fit" for their circumstances. I know these individuals probably represent the "tip of the iceberg," too.

CBS News aired a report on Aug. 28, 2015, about a widow who nearly lost everything she had because of some bad financial advice. The same report was uploaded on YouTube by the U.S. Department of Labor the following month. It told the story of Ethel Sprouse, 68, and how she lost almost $400,000 from her retirement account — money she couldn't afford to lose. She said her problems began when her husband began showing signs of Alzheimer's, and she knew that she would have to start making all the financial decisions. Making her situation worse, her mentally-challenged daughter fell ill with a lung disease requiring surgery. She turned to a friend who was also a financial advisor. She reasoned that this individual knew her family's situation and would steer them in the right direction. According to the news report, her stockbroker/advisor invested her money in high-risk stocks in spite of her instructions to "play it safe."[35]

"He knew we could not afford to lose principal," Ethel told reporters. "He knew that we needed income. He knew my husband was sick and that I had a mentally challenged daughter. He was the last person I would have thought would have mishandled my funds."

Ethel watched helplessly as the balance of the account declined further and further. She says she still worries today if she and her daughter will have enough money to live out their lives.

Looking at the camera, Ethel pleaded with viewers. "Don't sit back and think it happens to somebody else; it happens to everyday people."[36]

The woman's investments may have been good for a single 25-year-old, or even for someone in their 40s with kids entering college. But for a retiree who would have to depend on her savings to see her through, it was the wrong call. She said she felt "betrayed by her broker and by the system that was supposed to protect her."

Let's face it — even doctors who have sworn a Hippocratic Oath to "do no harm" (they still do that, don't they?) sometimes get it wrong. It is not always because they mean to do harm. They just make diagnoses without all the facts. Or they could be working under the influence of a particular school of thought that is based on bad science. Some doctors take a conservative approach while others tend to be more aggressive and use the latest medicines and therapies available. There is nothing wrong with getting a second

---

[35] "Wall Street opposes White House crackdown on financial advisors." Wyatt Andrews. CBSNews. Aug. 28, 2015. http://www.cbsnews.com/news/wall-street-combats-white-house-crackdown-on-financial-advisors/.

[36] "Working to Protect Your Retirement Savings: Ethel Sprouse's Story." Department of Labor. Sept. 2, 2015. https://www.youtube.com/watch?v=K-jV-tVAmDY.

opinion, especially if surgery is involved. No doctor will object to that if he or she is a true professional.

When it comes to financial diagnoses, I tell people, if you don't feel comfortable with your financial plan, get a second opinion.

When it comes to financial planning, there is no such thing as a one-size-fits-all, cookie-cutter solution. Drew and I have had many conversations around the conference table with couples who were sold a "financial retirement product," when what they needed was help devising a plan customized to their individual needs.

I like to use the example of a shoe salesperson.

You: I would like to buy a pair of shoes, please.
Salesperson: Here try these. They are on sale.
You: But they are size 8. I wear size 10.
Salesperson: You will be fine with these. They're the latest thing.
You: But I need running shoes. These are high heels.
Salesperson: Will that be cash or charge?

Crazy, right? Of course! As the prison warden (Strother Martin) said to the character played by Paul Newman in "Cool Hand Luke": "What we got here is failure to communicate!" If your shoes don't fit your feet, what good are they (the shoes, I mean)? In fact, wearing ill-fitting shoes for a long period of time could cripple the wearer!

"If you think professional advice is expensive, wait until you follow advice from an amateur."
~Anonymous

When people are sold financial products that don't fit their unique financial circumstances, it can lead to devastating circumstances. This is why, for a financial plan to be viable, it must take into consideration every aspect of your life and be tailor-made to the purpose you see for your wealth.

Whom Can You Trust?

When it comes to financial advice, whom can you trust? If you type the words "financial advice" into your computer's search engine, more than 7 million responses will pop up in less than a second. It seems that everyone wants to advise you on what to do with your money these days.

Last year I found myself in a shopping mall with my wife, Andrea. While she visited the stores, I made my way to a large bookstore to browse the shelves. One entire wall was devoted to financial books and magazines. There were hundreds of books and scores of periodicals, all offering financial advice. Magazines with bold headlines competed for my attention as I walked past them on the crowded racks.

"Top Ten Mutual Funds You Can't Afford to Miss"

"Seven Secrets Smart Investors Know"

"Why The Dollar's Next Move Will Be Lower"

"Get in Emerging Market ETFs Now!"

"How to Take Advantage of Falling Oil Prices"

It was enough to make you dizzy.

A tsunami of financial advice is coming at us from all directions these days. We are inundated with conflicting opinions. Cable television has several financial channels. They often have two "experts" on a split screen, each bickering with the other about why the stock market moved in whatever direction it did that day. Such on-screen back and forth may be good for ratings, but it is downright confusing to the viewing public.

Because of the greed on Wall Street, trust is a real issue. The events of the 2008 financial crisis and the bank bailouts are still fresh in investors' minds. So are the crooked schemes pulled off by Bernie Madoff and others. It is no wonder that people tend to gravitate to friends, relatives and co-workers — people they know — for financial advice. The problem is, you may be able to trust good ol' Uncle George with your life, but he probably doesn't know what he is talking about when he gives you financial advice (no offense if you have a real uncle named George).

Every large office has what I call the "water cooler financial advisor" who loves to give his co-workers stock tips on the next "sure thing" on Wall Street. And, of course, there are always a few who are drawn to such advice, seeking to strike it rich with the next Google or Apple. These folks are also well-meaning but usually misguided.

The one that kills me, and the most dangerous of all, is the guy who comes on one of the major financial channels with his sleeves rolled up, wearing a clown hat, yelling at the screen as if he's always angry. He then proceeds to issue market predictions and stock picks as if he is some kind of clairvoyant who knows what the market will do before it does it. When he is right (which he sometimes is), he punctuates his victory with a zoom whistle and a loud bulb horn. When he is wrong (which he often is), you never hear a peep. It would be good comedy (which is all it is) if it weren't for the fact that some people use their hard-earned money to follow his advice and end up losing money they cannot afford to lose.

So that's the problem. What is the solution?

Seek the Advice of a Fiduciary

Fiduciary. Now, there is a word we don't hear often in everyday conversation. Fid-DOO-she-airy. Sounds a little like an ice cream topping, doesn't it? The word fiduciary comes from the Latin word for trust. The legal definition is "a person to whom property or power is entrusted for the benefit of another." It may not be a common household word, but it is one you need to know if you are seeking financial advice.

I'm not the only one who thinks this. The U.S. Department of Labor thinks the same way. Here is the transcript from a whiteboard video entitled "Are Your Savings at Risk?" produced by the government to alert consumers to the dangers of not using a fiduciary when seeking financial counsel:[37]

Are Your Savings at Risk?

"How much should you be saving for retirement? And how should you do it? These are questions that everyday Americans, old and young alike, should be asking ourselves. If you don't know the answers to these questions, if you think saving for retirement is intimidating, and a little confusing to navigate, you're not alone. All of us need good advice on how to start saving our hard-earned money and how to make our nest eggs grow. That's why millions of people turn to a trusted financial advisor to help with these critical decisions. Just as we go to doctors when we are sick, or lawyers when we need legal help. But what you might not know is that, unlike doctors or lawyers, some financial advisors are not required to put your interests ahead of their own. While most advisors do put their customers' best interests first, others don't. So instead of doing what's best for you, they're serving themselves.

"We have a fix for this. A proposed federal rule from the Labor Department would require retirement advisors to put their client's interests first. In technical terms, that's called a fiduciary responsibility.

"Let's take a look at Lisa and Peggy. Lisa is 45 and she and her family have $100,000 in retirement savings. Investing with a fiduciary's advice, Lisa grew her savings to more than $216,000 over 20 years, adjusted for inflation. Now, let's take Peggy. Peggy's financial advisor put his interests first. Peggy's savings only grew to $179,000 — $37,000 less than Lisa's.

"That's right! Under our current system, your advisor can profit by steering you toward a more expensive investment, even if it is not the

---

[37] "White Board Explainer: Your Retirement Protections." From "Are Your Retirement Savings at Risk?" United States Department of Labor. Aug. 24, 2015. http://www.dol.gov/protectyoursavings/.

best one for you. There are stories of brokers being offered trips to Hawaii if they meet certain sales goals, even if their advice isn't best for their clients. You should expect your advisor to be thinking about your retirement security, not their tropical vacation.

"The costs of conflicted advice are huge — in fact, more than $17 billion a year by one estimate. But how are you supposed to know who you can trust? Outdated regulations, loopholes and the corrosive power of fine print make it hard to know. We are proposing that all financial advisors abide by a fiduciary, or best interest standard. In other words, they'd be required to put your best interests ahead of their own. You've worked hard for your money. You deserve the best advice. Advice that is in your best interests. Learn more about protecting your savings."

Safe Advisors vs. Risk Advisors

Let me start by saying most financial professionals with whom I am acquainted are OK people who are honest and well-intentioned. I certainly don't want to throw rocks at any of them. There are "safe money" advisors, and there are "risk" advisors. There is a place for both of these advisor "species" in the financial world, but it is important to understand the difference, especially if you are investing your retirement savings.

The "Safe" Side

Banks are very safe. As I am writing this, in the year of our Lord 2016, banks aren't paying a lot of interest on their savings accounts and CDs. This has not always been the case. Maybe you remember back in 1980 when we had double-digit inflation and banks were keeping pace. It was a double-edged sword. If you were a borrower, you paid 14-17 percent interest. If you were a saver, you received the same. The only problem was, prices and living costs were going up so fast that any gain you received from the banks was illusionary. You may have gained it on the income side, but you lost it on the outgoing side.

I was in the banking industry in those days. I remember when we had a run on our bank one day because our bank president decided to offer 14 percent interest on a money market account! We had to call the police for crowd control because so many people wanted to open an account with us that day.

It is a bit unfair, but those days are still referred to as the "Jimmy Carter" days of inflation. He was president then, but he just inherited the mess that President Richard M. Nixon created in the early 1970s with his wage- and price-freeze legislation.

Nowadays, bank CDs are nicknamed "certificates of disappointment" because interest rates are so low. But when you think of safe money places, the banks are on top of the list. Banks and credit unions. Banks and savings and loan associations are insured by the FDIC (Federal Deposit Insurance Corporation) with limits of $250,000 per depositor, per bank. Federal credit unions are insured by the NCUA (National Credit Union Administration).

Banks were not always so rock solid. Before the creation of the FDIC, if a bank failed and your money was in it, you lost your money. The Great Depression saw so many bank failures in the 1930s that something had to be done if banks were going to continue to be a viable place for people to put their money. Many who survived that era were reluctant to ever trust banks again.

Also on the safe money side, you have insurance companies. Insurance products, such as life insurance, fixed annuities and fixed index annuities, operate under the "safe" banner because they promise no loss of principal. They are not insured by the FDIC or the NCUA. Insurance companies must provide their own safety net by means of maintaining large reserve funds. State laws in the various states in which the insurance companies are chartered require insurance companies to participate in guaranty associations that essentially assure the consumer that, if an insurance company goes belly up, its policyholders won't be left holding the bag.

The Risk Side

On the risk side are commission-based stockbrokers. They are paid a commission each time they make a trade in your portfolio. As everyone knows, risk is an inherent part of the stock market. When you buy shares of stock in a company, the value of those shares may soar, or they may sour, or they may remain the same. When the stock loses money, you, as a shareholder, participate in that loss. When the stock increases in value, you participate in that gain.

Let me go on record as saying there is nothing wrong with investment risk and there is nothing wrong with commissions. It is all part of the American free enterprise system. When we are invested in the stock market, we do not begrudge either risk or commission as long as what? As long as we are making money! It's when we lose money that we may hold a measure of disdain for those two things.

You also have what are called "fee-only advisors." A fee advisor gets paid no commission. They charge a fee to manage your money. Bankers and fee-only advisors are legally required to act as fiduciaries. Their advice must be free of personal interest and solely in the best interests of their clients.

Stockbrokers and insurance agents are held to the less restrictive suitability standard.

Fiduciary vs. Suitability

These days it is easy to hang out a shingle and declare yourself a "financial advisor," even if you have no SEC registration (That's Securities and Exchange Commission, not Southeastern Conference). You could even work for a company that markets very few financial products and requires that you sell only those products. I am not saying these salespeople are out to harm folks, but if their advice has to be wrapped around just a few financial products, whether they be insurance products, such as life insurance or annuities, or mutual funds and stocks and bonds, there is no way it can be custom tailored for your financial needs and goals for the future.

That's where the difference between fiduciary and suitability standards comes in. Suitability, even though the word itself carries a positive connotation, is the lesser of these two standards. One may conclude that if advice is "suitable" that it would be in your best interests. That is not necessarily true in the world of finance, however, where "suitability" leaves the door open for a possible conflict of interests. Investment brokers who work for a broker-dealer are obligated to represent the firm, not the client.

Think of real estate agents. They put the buyer and seller together. That doesn't mean they are working against the buyer or the seller's best interest. But it would be naïve to think they are working solely for the best interests of either party.

The need to disclose potential conflicts of interest is not as strict a requirement for brokers. An investment recommendation can be suitable without being consistent with the investor's financial profile and objectives. Stockbrokers may recommend an investment if it is suitable for their client. What does that mean? If it is a stock, they should be asking you about your risk tolerance, for example, before they recommend an investment that could cause you to lose a lot of money if the stock were to lose value. If it is a mutual fund, they should openly discuss the fees and loads associated with the fund. If there is more than one investment that is "suitable" for you, brokers are within their legal rights to recommend the one that offers them the most profit, and they are not obligated to tell you that they are making more money by providing that investment over another, if both investments are deemed "suitable." While this is technically ethical and legal, it is not how most of us want to be dealt with.

In case you are wondering, Drew and I are Investment Advisor Representatives, which means we must adhere to the higher fiduciary standard that legally binds us by law to offer only what is in the best interest of the client. Of course, we are financially remunerated for our work, but it is never a consideration when advising clients. Those chips fall where they may.

You may also be wondering where the fiduciary standard originated. It was established as part of the Investment Advisors Act of 1940 and is regulated by the Securities and Exchange Commission or state securities regulators.

In some commercial settings, you pay extra for better service. Take air travel for example. If you want to fly first class or business class as opposed to coach, you will pay extra. The same goes for a private hospital room or a luxury suite at a fancy hotel. But by law, you pay nothing extra for the services of a fiduciary.

The easiest way to know if you are working with a fiduciary is just to ask.

"Excuse me, but are you working on the fiduciary standard or the suitability standard?"

If they don't know what either of those are, you may be in the wrong place.

Do we believe that all investment brokers are unethical? Not at all! Quite the opposite is true. The ones we know personally are ethical and honest. We are simply saying that fiduciary financial advisors do not work for a large brokerage house. They do not work from a "menu" of products. They are usually independent and in a position to offer many strategies and approaches to help their clients achieve their goals.

"How Do You Get Paid?"

We are taught from an early age not to ask such rude questions as "How much do you earn?" But asking your financial advisor *how* he or she gets paid is not rude. It's a good way to sniff out whether you are working with a fiduciary. This is your money, after all. You want to know ASAP if there is a conflict of interest between you and your advisor.

Commission is not a dirty word. Think of a travel agent. They can usually save you lots of money if you are taking a two-week vacation in the Caribbean. Why? Because they can shop for the best price on hotels and airlines. They don't work for any of the vendors they use to put a travel package together for you. But are they compensated by the airlines and hotels they use? Absolutely. You don't mind because you are the one who benefits in the long run.

In the investing world, it violates both the suitability and the fiduciary standard if a stockbroker misuses his or her relationship with the client by "churning" — that is trading in excess within a portfolio just to earn extra commissions. And yet it goes on. The best clues to tell if it is happening to you is by examining the statement from your brokerage firm. They are required to send you confirmations of every transaction. If you notice an excess of trading activity, ask about it.

Taking Ownership of Your Decisions

I know it may sound corny, but I got into the financial services business because I wanted to help people. Coming up with solutions and strategies to help people find success in retirement is like solving a puzzle. Finding the pieces that fit together and make their vision of the future come into focus. Most days, I have too much fun and satisfaction to call what I do work. But there are times I have experienced deep frustration when there are some problems I have not been able to solve.

Shortly after the 2008 market crash, a couple came into my office, and I could tell they were upset almost to the point of tears. We will call them John and Mary for confidentiality purposes. Their situation is typical of many I saw in the months that followed those dismal days.

As I listened to them tell their story, it was easy to see why they were upset. He was 63, and she was 62, and they had put their blood, sweat and tears into a nursery business they had started from scratch shortly after they were married.

They were a good team. John loved to tinker and Mary found pleasure in seeing things grow. Their business blossomed and did especially well when the housing market thrived because they supplied contractors with shrubs, trees, sod and other landscaping needs. They developed a reputation for great customer service. John and Mary were the types of business people who bent over backward to make sure their customers were happy. They and their business prospered.

As is so often the case, however, they were so involved in making their business a success that they neglected to properly look after their own personal finances. They put most of the money back into their business. They called it "re-seeding." Their business was debt-free and earned a solid profit. Money they didn't need to live on, they put in the hands of a financial advisor in whom they had ultimate trust and did not think anything more about it. It never occurred to them to ask questions about their investments. As long as the numbers were up, John would usually glance at the statements he received from his broker and file them away.

John and Mary planned to retire when he reached 65. They would sign the nursery over to their two sons, who had learned the business quite well and were very dependable. John and Mary had plans to take a couple of years and tour the country in a motor home that they had their eye on. Running their business consumed so much of their time that they had put off traveling for three decades. But they figured they would make up for lost time once they retired. Mary had a special folder she called her "wish book." It contained touring maps and brochures of national parks and other points of interest they intended to visit.

When the stock market crashed in 2008, they lost more than half their nest egg. They were stunned. Their broker said he was sorry, but there was nothing anyone could do. The money was just gone. "Just hang in there," he told them. "It will come back."

Attempting to console them, he told the couple that others had lost lots of money in the market crash. "These things happen from time to time," he had said.

Sitting there at the conference table with them, I felt like a first responder at a crash site. All I could do was help them stop the bleeding and get them back on solid ground with what was left of their portfolio. There was no fixing the fact that John and Mary would have to postpone their retirement for at least another three or four years. They would survive because they had been frugal and had no debt. But they would have no choice but to continue working.

Toward the end of our conversation, Mary said, "I just wish John and I had paid more attention and asked more questions about how they were investing our money."

I nodded in agreement. She was right, of course. They should have paid more attention. Their advisor had obviously not invested with their age and their retirement goals in mind. Trusting your financial advisor is a good thing, but blind trust is never a good thing. They should have asked questions until they fully understood the investment strategies that had been implemented on their behalf, and understood all the "what ifs" that were associated with them.

We are captains of our own financial ship. We may employ others to help us navigate, but at the end of the day, no one will care as much about our financial well-being as we. Ask questions until you have satisfied your curiosity and then ask one more: "Are there any questions that I need to ask, but haven't?"

CHAPTER NINE

Constructing Your Financial House

"It is not the beauty of a building you should look at; it's the construction of the foundation that will stand the test of time." ~ David Allan Coe

Folks in central Florida still talk about the "Groundhog Day" tornado outbreak that swept across the state in the middle of the night of Feb. 2, 2007, virtually erasing entire neighborhoods just a few miles from where the Blackston families now live and work. By the time we moved to the sunshine state in 2009, most of the homes had been rebuilt just as they were before the twisters hit. Why? Because even though the tornados had turned the upper portion of some houses to splinters, the concrete slab foundations of those structures were still intact.

When we moved here, I learned that most Florida houses are built on concrete slab foundations. This is because of the shallow water table, mainly, and the warm, humid climate. I also learned there is a lot more to these foundations than meets the eye. Most of them have a ribbon of steel-reinforced concrete 18 inches wide and two feet deep around their perimeters. Inside, the concrete is between four and six inches thick with more steel or fiber reinforcement. That's why they are so strong. The house may be blown completely away, but if the foundation is intact, the upper structure can be easily rebuilt.

Financial Foundations

With financial houses, everything rests on the foundation. It is the most important element of the building. Lay the foundation properly or the rest of the plan could fall apart. Safety is the key word. The foundation must be stable, capable of producing incomes that are reliable, predictable and impervious to the vagaries of a volatile stock market and the whirlwinds of economic change. What comes to mind? Certificates of deposit, savings accounts, pensions, fixed annuities, Social Security. We want sources of income that will still be there if (when) we have another market crash like the one that occurred in 2008. These income sources must at the very least cover your household expenses in retirement. Food, clothing, shelter, transportation and health care.

This is where the aforementioned Rule of 100 comes in. In case you missed the definition of this rule of thumb earlier, simply take your age and subtract it from 100 — that's the amount you should have absolutely safe from loss of principle. You could say that your age and your risk tolerance will tell you how thick the foundation of your financial house needs to be.

Again this is a rule of **thumb**. The expression "rule of thumb" means approximate. Ancient builders measured an inch from the tip of the thumb to the first joint — thus the term. Likewise, one person's financial foundation will not exactly mirror that of another. The principle, however, remains. For example, if you are retired and in your 70s, which will concern you the most? Your rate of return, or protecting your savings from loss? Obviously, the latter. The opposite is true with youngsters just starting out. Time is on their side, and they should take on more risk with their investments. From where I watch the world of saving and investing, too many young people fail to take advantage of the investing principle of the Rule of 100 (too many expensive toys), and I see too much risk taken on by retirees and those on the threshold of retirement.

I have also seen what I call the "catch up" syndrome. That's when seniors lose a chunk of their retirement savings in a market downturn (because they were too much at risk), and then they try to make up their losses by taking on even more risk in the stock market. In Las Vegas, they call this "doubling down" — shoving all their chips on the line hoping for the big win. We both know that such gambles rarely pay off. Those folks need to remember they are no longer in their accumulation years. Their age and station in life dictate they be more cautious with their assets.

The Walls of Your Financial House

Once we have our foundation (safe, secure sources of income) in place, now we can build the walls of our financial house (moderate risk investments to fill in the income gaps). We will get to the roof in just a moment.

During the Florida housing boom of the early 2000s, when new single-family houses were popping up like daisies after a spring rain, some contractors began using inferior drywall that was manufactured in China. It was cheap and plentiful. Problems developed, however, when new homeowners began sniffing a rotten-egg smell a few months after they moved in. Apparently, the wallboard consisted of a material that had a high sulfur content. A big class action lawsuit ensued and many builders went bankrupt when the claims started rolling in.

The point is after you get the solid foundation in place, start putting up the walls of your financial house. Your objective now is to fill in the gaps between the income produced by your foundation and other expenses that may not all be considered essential, but are desirable, such as travel, helping with the grandkids' education, or providing a legacy for heirs. The walls should consist of investments with the potential for good, solid returns without sacrificing too much safety.

Your walls may consist of alternative investments that are not directly tied to Wall Street, but capable of respectable returns without market risk. Corporate bonds and limited partnerships are a good example. Other nonmarket investments could be Real Estate Investment Trusts, or REITs. These are companies that own (and usually operate) real estate properties that are capable of generating income. Hotels, condominiums, shopping centers, self-storage units. All of these and more could be part of a Real Estate Investment Trust.

Here is where you must exercise caution. There are two kinds of REITs — publicly traded REITs and privately traded REITs. Publicly traded REITs are liquid, just like stocks or ETFs (exchange traded funds). Buy it today at a certain share price, sell it tomorrow at the going rate. Privately traded REITs, since they are not listed on a stock exchange, are not as liquid. You put your money in today, and it may be a long time before you get it back.

Before purchasing a REIT, make sure you understand the fees involved, the potential downside and the illiquidity factor. As the calendar puts more distance between us and the real estate crash of 2007, memory fades of share prices dropping from $10 to $4 virtually overnight.

All I am saying is, be careful of the materials with which you build the walls of your financial house. Not all alternative investments (not based in the stock market), are suitable for retirees.

What's that? Why do I see so many illiquid, privately traded REITs in the portfolios of retirees and those getting ready to retire? One word, starts with C. Commissions on REITs can run as high as 10 percent!

The Roof

The roof is the part of the house that gets the brunt of bad weather. It is also like that with our financial house. The roof is where we want our high-risk, high-reward assets. The roof may be the first to take a hit, but it represents the potential for the biggest gain from the stock market.

Using the Rule of 100 as a guide, you will not have so much of your nest egg in harm's way as to cause you financial ruin. One key point to remember is that the roof is put in place only *after* you have guaranteed income in place for the rest of your life and moderate-risk, alternative nonmarket investments in place to balance out the risk. The roof of your financial house is exposed to all manner of events you cannot control — natural disasters, terrorist attacks, sudden economic wind gusts — all of which can do financial damage. But because you have the appropriate amount invested here, the risk is worth the reward. Typically, traditional investments go here — stocks, mutual funds or even variable annuities in some cases. Again, no financial plan should be like another. Everyone has different goals, dreams, aspirations and sensitivity to risk.

Comfortable Financial Houses

Your financial house needs to fit your lifestyle. Just as your personal home reflects your taste and preferences in everything from the color of the cabinets to the type of windows you select, your financial house should be custom built to your specifications — not some prefabricated house that is stamped out without consideration of your unique circumstances. Only a skilled and caring architect can provide the design that is just right for you.

Here's a good example of what I'm talking about: A couple who eventually became our clients had enough money to live a lavish lifestyle and own a much larger home than the one in which they lived. But they were conservative people, happy with their relatively modest lifestyle. They have three children and nine grandchildren, whom they enjoy immensely. They both feel a strong obligation to pass on a solid legacy to their family. They live comfortably, but the one great comfort in their financial lives is the knowledge that they are building a protective financial wall around those they love.

This is where having a financial architect comes in — one who will take the time to ask enough questions, digest the answers, and then design a plan that is a comfortable fit. In this case, the husband and wife were both very healthy. They were delighted (and pleasantly surprised) to learn that a strategy involving life insurance could be used to provide a legacy for their children, and offer them living benefits as well. Second-to-die life policies are often used in estate planning when the goal is to pass along as much as possible to children or grandchildren in the most tax-efficient manner possible. Such policies provide for children to become the beneficiaries after the last surviving spouse dies. They were able to leave $1 million to their kids completely **tax free!** These folks were well educated and intelligent, but they did not know such a strategy existed. Once their legacy goal was in place, the couple told me they felt much better about enjoying some of the money they had worked so hard to accumulate.

From left, Drew and David Blackston.

CHAPTER TEN

Treat Your Health Like Your Wealth

"The only way to keep your health is to eat what you don't want, drink what you don't like, and do what you'd rather not." ~ Mark Twain

As I said at the beginning of this book, it's the little decisions we make along the way through life that come back to either bless or haunt us. For example, ignoring health warnings can lead to illness and even early death. I know of one man who bragged that he had never been to a doctor. I didn't really know him; I just met him in a clubhouse after a golf game. The man appeared to be in his early 60s, and he did look fit.

"Not even for a checkup?" I asked.

"Nope, not even for a checkup," he said, adding with a chuckle, "The way I look at it, if it ain't broke, don't fix it."

I wanted to say, but did not out of politeness, "Good luck with that."

I never encountered him again and always wondered how that attitude toward taking care of his physical health worked out for him.

It is just plain foolish to ignore our health, especially after we pass the half-century mark. The annual physical exam should be automatic and non-negotiable for anyone who qualifies for senior movie tickets, membership in AARP or a discount on coffee at the local McDonald's. All of us know someone, or, at least, we know someone who knows someone, who passed away well before his or her time due to some easily preventable disease. Cancer comes to mind. With so many screening techniques in place these days, early detection and effective treatment are often a ticket to a long and happy life.

Some people are as cavalier about their finances as the guy I ran into in the clubhouse. They either attempt to go the do-it-yourself route, or they entrust their financial well-being to advisors who are either unqualified or unethical. All I'm saying is treat your wealth like your health. Pay attention to it, and seek the counsel of a fully trained professional who is a fiduciary and has your best interest at heart.

Doctor Blackston, I Presume?

How would you feel about this scenario? You are new to the area, and someone recommends me as your doctor. You come to my office. You have your medical history in one hand and the medications you are currently taking in the other.

"Hello. I am Dr. Blackston. How are you doing? What's that you have in your hand? Medical records? Nah, I don't need to see your medical records, and I don't need to know what medicine you are taking. I'm not going to weigh you, or listen to your heart. Nothing like that. But you know what? Just looking at you, I think you need to be on Crestor immediately. Here, let me just write you out a prescription and you can be on your way."

How would you feel about me as a doctor?

Exactly. Run, don't walk, as far away from that quack as possible.

Looking at Tax Returns

So, why is it that some will let their financial advisor make recommendations on investments and never ask questions or look at their tax return? That's why so many people are paying unnecessary taxes. Their advisors made recommendations without checking to see how it would affect them, tax-wise.

Let me give you a good example. A couple of years ago a husband and wife came into my office. They were 75 and 73 years old, respectively. They had just been to one of our public education events and had heard me talking about taxes. During this part of the program, I try to make it clear that, while I don't necessarily *enjoy* paying taxes, I do view it as my civic and patriotic duty. I want to pay every penny of tax I owe; I just don't want to pay one penny more! Don't get me wrong, I love my country as much as the next guy, but I pay a lot in taxes. I don't feel required to donate to Uncle Sam any more money than he requires of me. Maybe that's how this couple felt. Maybe that explains why they brought with them their tax records for the past three years. They also brought financial statements from their investment portfolios, but they were particularly interested in taxes.

"I just feel like we are paying more than we need to," said the woman.

When I looked at their taxes, I noticed they had incurred more than $400,000 in losses back in 2008 when the stock market crashed and their advisor pulled them out of the market. As most people know, you are only allowed to write off $3,000 in capital losses each year on your taxes if you don't have gains in other investments that offset those losses.

I had to ask: "Tell me, was your advisor that you are working with now the same one who lost this money for you back in '08?"

"Oh yes," the woman said. "He is such a sweet gentleman. He is like one of our kids."

"Just out of curiosity, have you named him as a beneficiary in your will?" I was joking of course, but there was a measure of seriousness in the question. She smiled a wry smile, realizing that perhaps she had been making business decisions out of sentiment and that it may have cost them a small fortune.

What was the issue here? They had unrealized gains in their investment portfolio. They had bought stocks and mutual funds at a low value. The shares had since increased in value. When I asked them why they had not sold these assets, they told me their advisor had informed them they would have in excess of $250,000 in gains, which would result in huge capital gains taxes.

"Did your advisor look at these tax returns?" I asked.

The couple shook their heads in unison. "No," said the woman. "That's one of the reasons we are here."

I said, "If I can show you a way you can sell the gains, offset them with those losses, and it costs you nothing to do this — no taxes — and if you like the investments you're in, we'll turn right around and buy them back, would a strategy like that be of interest to you?

"Yes, but how can that work?" asked the husband.

"You can do that on a gain; you just can't do that on a loss," I explained, and showed them the chapter and verse of the provision in the IRS code that applied to their situation. They have been clients ever since, and they bring their tax return with them to each annual review.

Taxes on Social Security

One of the proudest moments in the presidency of Franklin D. Roosevelt was in 1935 when he signed the Social Security Act into law. I wasn't there, so I can't say for sure if it really happened, but the story goes that when reporters asked him if he would ever **tax** Social Security benefits, he pounded his fist on the oval office desk and vowed, "I will **never** tax Social Security!" I suppose you could say that FDR kept that promise. Social Security benefits weren't taxed while he was alive. For that matter, they remained untaxed for another 48 years.

Under President Ronald Reagan, however, the Social Security Amendments of 1983 was passed. The new law said that if your annual base income was $25,000 as a single taxpayer, or $32,000 for a married couple filing jointly, then up to 50 percent of your Social Security income would be taxed as ordinary income. Next came the 1993 budget deal under President Bill Clinton, requiring that taxation apply to 85 percent of benefits for single beneficiaries with incomes over $34,000 and couples over $44,000.

The key as to whether you will pay taxes on Social Security is how much **reportable** income you have. What is considered **reportable** income? Just about everything: income from investments, interest from CDs, pensions, brokerage accounts and even tax-free income.

Wait a minute! You mean that I could have just enough money sitting in a bank CD to generate $100 in interest, and that $100 could kick my Social Security check into the "taxable" category? Yes. Happens all the time!

You mean that I could have dividends from a brokerage account, and even if I reinvest the money back into the account, and never spent it, that dividend could trigger a tax on my Social Security benefits?

Yes, indeed! Even if you never actually touched the money. That is why it is sometimes called "phantom income."

Some folks, when they prepare their taxes, just fill in the boxes on their 1040 form, unaware that there are ways to ethically and legally avoid the Social Security tax (sometimes called the senior-only tax). The IRS allows you to reposition some of your assets into accounts where income generated from the account is nonreportable. In some cases, it is deemed tax free by the IRS, and in other cases, taxes are deferred until you actually withdraw the funds. Take U.S. Savings Bonds, for example. You buy them for, say, $50, and, if you keep them long enough, they mature to $100. You don't pay taxes on that money until you actually cash in the bond. Same goes for tax-deferred annuities. Moving income-producing assets from the reportable category to the nonreportable category is a way to legally, ethically and honestly avoid taxation on Social Security benefits.

What I am telling you is not secret. Guess who publishes these provisions in great detail? The Internal Revenue Service. According to the Tax Foundation, an independent tax policy research organization, the IRS tax code contains 70,000 pages and more than a million words. But there is no section entitled "Tips on Avoiding Unnecessary Taxation," or "20 Popular Tax Breaks." They are there, but you have to know where to look.

Let me give you another good example. A few years ago, probably back in 2004 or 2005, we had a couple come in who were both in their early 80s. They've since passed away, but here was their situation: They had Social Security income and a little more coming in from a mortgage contract they carried when they sold their farm. Their interest income, which amounted to around $43,000 per year, was just enough to kick their Social Security over into the 85 percent taxable bracket.

"How much of the interest income do you actually need to live on?" I asked.

"We don't need any of that money," was their reply. "We have no debt and we live comfortably on our Social Security income."

The couple had no children. I knew this because we had helped them set up a trust to avoid probate.

"If I could show you a way to lower your taxes and give you more income, would you at least want to see it?" I asked them. They said yes.

All we did was find a nonreportable category into which we put the interest income that was triggering the tax on their Social Security. A year or so later, when tax season rolled around, I received a phone call from the couple's CPA. He asked me where the $43,000 interest income went. He was accustomed to just filling in the same blanks from last year, and this year the $43,000 wasn't there. All we did was move the $43,000 into a perfectly legitimate, nonreportable, tax-deferred account.

To make sure there was no confusion, I made a trip to his office and sat down with him and the couple and carefully went through the steps we had taken. When we were finished, he said to me with an earnest expression, "Why didn't someone explain this to these people four years ago when they sold the property? It would have eliminated all those taxes they had been paying for those four years."

The bottom line? If you are working with a financial advisor who does not take the time to look at your tax return, you may be working with the wrong advisor.

Check Those Beneficiaries

More and more financial products and investment accounts come with beneficiary designations these days. Naming a beneficiary is one of the most important pen strokes you will make. The reason these products/accounts come with named beneficiary options is clear. When the owner of the account dies, the assets pass on to the named beneficiary — in many cases without the interference of a costly and lengthy probate process. Please make sure the name on the beneficiary line agrees with your overall estate plan. Named beneficiaries on an account nearly always supersede provisions of a will.

A couple — we will call them David and Andrea — came to one of our educational events where this topic was discussed. They followed up with an appointment, the purpose of which was to have us check the beneficiary designations on a number of their financial documents. One was a life insurance policy. We called the company and received permission from the couple to ask questions on their behalf. We put the conversation on speakerphone.

"Can you please tell me who the primary beneficiary of this insurance policy is?" I asked. The policy had a face amount of $50,000.

The person on the other end of the phone told me the name. We will call her Sally.

I muted the phone. "Who is Sally?" I asked

"His ex-wife," said Andrea quickly.

"What is she still doing on this policy?" said her husband.

Things ended well in this case. We requested a change of beneficiary form from the insurance company. David, the insured, and owner of the policy, was able to update the information.

Believe it or not, mistakes such as this one are common. People take out life insurance policies. Years go by. Life happens. People get divorced and remarried. Children come along. Then grandchildren. If the information on the policy is not current, thousands of dollars can pass on to — there's no other way to put it — the wrong people! It is critically important to make sure the beneficiary lines on investment accounts. It is not unusual to see 401(k) and other retirements to grow by hundreds of thousands of dollars with outdated information on the beneficiary lines.

Two young women whose mother had recently died came to see us one afternoon with estate questions. Their mother had died, leaving them $2.1 million in bank CDs. The estate had to go through probate, a process that ended up costing the estate around $100,000. All of this could have been avoided, and the money transferred to the girls 50/50, without the hassle and expense of probate, had their mother added a POD, or payable on death, provision to the CD.

When people change jobs, they sometimes are under the mistaken impression that if they roll a 401(k) plan to an IRA or their new employer's retirement plan, the beneficiary they listed on their old plans rolls over with it. Not so. You have to name a beneficiary each time.

Did you know that most bank accounts can be made POD (payable on death) just like life insurance policies? Stocks, bonds and mutual funds are TOD (transferred on death) to named beneficiaries.

Beneficiaries can be single individuals, trusts, charities, churches, civic organizations, groups of people. They can be specifically named or designated simply as "all my children who survive me," or "all my grandchildren."

We know of cases where hurt feelings were caused when a person with multiple accounts tried to put a different son or daughter as beneficiary on each account. Some received more than others, and relationships were damaged as a result.

Some forms won't allow you to pass your assets "per stirpes," a legal term which means "equally to the branches of your family." Let's say, for example, that you list your four adult children as your beneficiaries to your IRA account. Should one die before you do, you may wish for that son or daughter's share to go to his or her grandchildren. Sometimes the form has a cramped space with one line on which to designate the beneficiary. Don't be intimidated by this. It is a document. You may need to seek some professional help doing this, but it is perfectly legal to express yourself thoroughly and in great detail. Use as much paper and as many staples as you need. That's why they are there.

In these matters, never assume the people on the other side of the desk are going to volunteer all the information you need to know. They may not be out to deceive you. It could be that they don't know. As the saying goes, "If it is to be, it is up to thee." It's your money and your family. Ask questions and make sure you are comfortable with the answers you get. Oh, and please make copies of everything and put them in a fire-proof safe. You can buy them at big variety stores for under $200.

Look at the Positive

Stress is not only a mental burden, but medical science has proven that stress can lead to many physical breakdowns. According to WebMD, stress can play a part in causing headaches, high blood pressure, heart problems, diabetes, skin conditions, asthma, arthritis, depression and anxiety. All that from stress!

All our financial problems won't be solved in a day, or even a year, but our mental approach to these problems can start right now. Look at the blessings in your life. Is your family healthy? Do you have a roof over your head? Focus on the things that you love in your life. When you make the decision to stop looking at your problems and start focusing on solutions, you make a U-turn on the highway of stress and anxiety. An old proverb says, "Whoever pursues goodness and love finds life, prosperity and honor."

Financial stress is something each individual is faced with. We are bombarded on a daily basis to acquire, consume and even save more and more. Sometimes, these stress triggers can cause serious mental anguish and even physical illness. Life is short. Don't let worry, anxiety and stress steal the positives in your life. Take the small steps now to a brighter financial future![38]

---

[38] Joseph Goldberg. WebMD. June 24, 2014. "The Effects of Stress on Your Body." http://www.webmd.com/balance/stress-management/effects-of-stress-on-your-body.

CHAPTER ELEVEN

What's the Deal With Annuities?

"No one's ever achieved financial fitness with a January resolution that's abandoned by February." ~ Suze Orman

In my opinion, no other single financial instrument is as polarizing and more misunderstood as the annuity. It seems that half the people swear *at* them and the other half swears *by* them — especially among financial professionals.

If you go by the sales figures, a lot of people are putting their money in them. LIMRA, an insurance research organization, reports that total sales of all annuities in the U.S. amounted to $235.8 billion in 2014, "thanks to record annual sales ($42.8 billion) in indexed and income annuities."[39]

So, what's the deal? Why the love 'em or hate 'em thing? Let's start at the beginning, shall we?

---

[39] LIMRA Secure Retirement Institute. 2014. "Fourth Quarter 2014 U.S. Annuity Sales Survey."

History of Annuities

Back in the days of the Roman Empire, contracts known as *annua* provided annual payments to families of soldiers who had fallen in battle. The idea spread to Roman citizens at large, who would make a single payment to a money-lender in exchange for a promise of a lifetime of regular payments if they reached a certain age.

In Europe, in the 17ᵗʰ century, governments created *tontines* that paid out money (income) for an extended future period, years later, if citizens would purchase the contracts that day. Britain launched one of the first group annuities (State Tontine of 1663) as a way of funding their war with France.

In America, in 1759, a company in Pennsylvania established a fund to benefit Presbyterian ministers and their families. The ministers would pay small amounts into the fund in exchange for the promise of lifetime payments when they retired.

In 1812, the Pennsylvania Company for Insurance on Lives and Granting Annuities was the first company to offer annuities to the public. Annuities were used during the Civil War by the Union to compensate soldiers. President Abraham Lincoln endorsed an annuity plan to help families of veterans with war-related disabilities.

The concept of the annuity really started to catch on in the 1930s after the onset of the Great Depression. People turned to insurance companies as a haven for their cash when banks began failing, and they had lost confidence in the stock market.[40]

From Simple to Complex

Annuities, like many financial concepts, have evolved over the years. They remind me of automobiles in this regard. Are automobiles quieter, sleeker and more powerful than those of yesteryear? Absolutely! But have they also become more complex? Yes, indeed!

---

[40] Mark P. Cussen. Investopedia. "Introduction to Annuities: The History of Annuities." http://www.investopedia.com/university/annuities/.

Back when I started driving, automobiles were pretty simple and relatively easy to work on. Nowadays, on the rare occasions when I look under the hood of my car, I don't know what I'm looking at. I leave it to the professionals down at the dealership. They have specialized computers that talk to the computers on the car's engine. Can you imagine how Henry Ford would react if he could see what they have done with his simple idea?

So, just like cars, annuities these days are better, and they do more, but they are also more complex. In my opinion, that is one of the reasons they sometimes get bad press in the media. Reporters who couldn't answer five very basic questions about annuities presume to write lengthy editorials about them.

When I read one of these articles, I can usually tell in three or four paragraphs if they know what they are talking about, and many of them don't. They haven't done, as we like to say in the financial world, their "due diligence" before passing judgment. The most egregious pieces seem to be written by reporters who prefer to deal in sound bites instead of sound facts and are quick to quote pundits who know less than they do about the subject at hand.[41]

Categories of Annuities

Some of the financial instruments that come under the heading of "annuities" are so diverse that there should really be another name for them. It's like the term "motor vehicle." Under that broad heading, you have motorcycles, tractor-trailer rigs, passenger cars, sports cars and off-road dune buggies. Then, under the heading of passenger cars, you have Chevrolets, Fords, Chryslers, Toyotas, Nissans, and on and on.

There are many variations of annuities and each is dramatically different in how they function from their cousins.

---

[41] Ibid.

Take the variable annuity for example. Variable annuities were first unveiled in 1952, and they contained many new features. Variable annuities, or VAs, are stock market investments with an insurance twist. The idea was to allow mutual funds to grow tax deferred. If the market flourished, you didn't mind paying the fees associated with fund management and mutual funds in general. If the market tanked, yes, you could lose your initial investment, but one of the bells and whistles of the VA was a life insurance provision that allowed the amount you originally invested to go to your heirs at your death. That is a nutshell definition, but you can see how far afield that concept had strayed from the old-fashioned fixed annuity. And yet they are both "annuities."

Variable annuities are generally sold by stockbrokers. Fixed annuities are typically sold by insurance agents. You can lose your principal in variable annuities. Your principal is protected in fixed annuities.

So Uncle Bob has a few variable annuities in his portfolio with the brokerage house that manages his investments. The stock market takes a tumble, and he loses money across the board. He gets his variable annuity statement and sees those ugly parentheses that indicate a loss. He is hopping mad. He tells his wife, Florence, that he will never buy another annuity as long as he lives! Aunt Flo tells her sister, Jennie, who forms the opinion that all annuities are bad. In fact, when she hears the word, "annuity," she flinches and looks for two wooden pencils to make a cross with as if a vampire had just walked in the room. I exaggerate, of course, and it's meant to be amusing, but that's how people sometimes form opinions about things about which they know little or nothing.

There are few financial concepts out there that I go out of my way to unrecommend for folks in retirement, but the variable annuity is one of them. Apparently, I am not the only one. Suze Orman, in her book "The Road to Wealth," pulls no punches on VAs. On page 510, she relates a question put to her as follows: "My financial advisor is recommending that I buy a variable annuity within my retirement account. What should I do?" "Get yourself another financial advisor," she replies.

VA fees range between 3.5 percent and 5.5 percent of your account value per year. So if you have 6.5 percent growth, and your VA costs 5.5 percent, then your return shrinks to a measly 1 percent.

Why so many fees? Variable annuities have sub accounts similar to mutual funds, and they have administration fees. You may also pay rider fees, mortality fees and other charges.

Traditional Fixed Annuities

Having changed little over the years, traditional fixed annuities seem boringly simple and straightforward. They are generally regarded as a safe haven for money, just like a bank CD, but as I write this, traditional fixed annuities offer a fixed rate of return of more than double what bank certificates of deposits offer. Traditional fixed annuities provide lifetime income payouts or payouts for a set period.

You typically get a 10 percent free withdrawal per year, but you will pay a penalty if you take out more than that. Penalties usually start at 10 percent and decline until the surrender period (usually between seven and 10 years) expires.

That's a thumbnail sketch. Downside? When you opt to receive a payout, you must "annuitize" the contract. That means if you die two months after trading the balance of the account for a lifetime (or set period) payout, it's game over. Your heirs receive nothing. The insurance company keeps the rest of the money. For that reason, I have not been a big fan of them, either.

The Fixed Annuity "Makeover"

In the mid-1990s, when the stock market was on a tear, someone got a bright idea. It reminds me of that old commercial for Reese's Peanut Butter Cups. You know the one where they accidently stuck their chocolate bar in some peanut butter and discovered how tasty it was? Some actuaries must have gotten together and said, what would happen if we took the safety of the traditional fixed annuity and combined it with the growth potential of the stock market? And what if we eliminated the part where you had to annuitize the contract in order to generate a lifetime income? What if we made it so the heirs could receive the unused portion of the account when the owner died? And what if we made it so that, instead of a fixed interest rate, we allowed the upward movement of the stock market to dictate the returns? And if the market went down, the annuity didn't lose?

The product they came up with goes by several names — hybrid annuity, income annuity — but the one we hear most often, and the one the insurance industry prefers, is fixed index annuity, or FIA. To understand it better, let's take the name one word at a time:

- **FIXED** – The investor's money is not at risk in the stock market. The safety of the annuity is guaranteed by the insurance company and the guaranty association of the state where the insurance company does business. The annuitant owns a contract with the insurance carrier with guaranteed provisions.

- **INDEX** – The annuity's rate of interest is predicated on the performance of a stock market index, like the S&P 500, the NASDAQ, the Dow Jones or a combination of indices. When the index value goes up, so does your account value, usually up to a cap (or sometimes a spread). For example, if the index is up 20 percent, and your cap is 8 percent, you will get only an 8 percent return that year.

- **ANNUITY** – Despite the bells and whistles, it's still an annuity. Returns are tax-deferred, and the main feature is an annual payout in exchange for a lump sum deposit. Typically, taxes are only paid on these contracts when the owner withdraws the money. Other typical annuity features apply. Surrender periods are usually around 10–12 years with declining surrender charges until the 10–12 years expire and there are none. While you are in deferral, you are typically allowed to withdraw 10 percent from the contract annually without paying surrender penalties. Some FIAs allow for larger distributions than 10 percent if the owner is confined to a nursing home or is terminally ill. There is no penalty imposed for any size withdrawal once the contract has passed the surrender period.

Income Riders

According to the National Association for Fixed Annuities (NAFA), more than half of all FIAs purchased now include an **income rider.** They are called riders because they are optional and, although they don't cost a lot (around 1 percent of the annuity value per year), they aren't free. As to how they work, think of a sidecar and a motorcycle. A motorcycle can function independently of a sidecar, but not the other way around.

The income rider goes by many names, depending on which insurance carrier is involved:

GLWB – Guaranteed Lifetime Withdrawal Benefit

GLIB – Guaranteed Lifetime Income Benefit

GLIR – Guaranteed Lifetime Income Rider

You probably see a pattern here. The rider guarantees a lifetime income, usually of a set amount based on a formula set by the insurance company. It's not like the old-style annuitization, however. With income riders, if you trigger your income and then pass away six months later, your beneficiary receives the unused portion of the annuity.

Income riders vary from one company to another, but they all do essentially the same thing — provide a guaranteed income stream for life. There are more than a few moving parts with these "hybrid" annuities, or "income" annuities. Think of one account with two ledgers. One ledger is the **base account**. That's the account from which you may withdraw 10 percent of your money from each year without penalty. Then there is the **income account**, which you cannot access as a lump sum. Its sole purpose is to provide you payments, like a pension, over time.

Insurance companies have what they call a "roll-up" rate they use to determine how much is credited to your income account. Your age will determine how what percentage of the income account will flow to you as income. Naturally, the higher the value of your income account, and the older you are when you trigger the income, the higher your income will be.

It is important not to confuse the value of the *income* account with the *base* account. The base account is your *"walk-away"* money. That is to say, after the surrender period, you can walk away from the contract with that amount. The income account is used as a calculation base for income. That's all it does.

Moving Parts

These are all thumbnail sketches and abbreviated descriptions of these somewhat complex financial instruments. Some will read this part of the book and say, "This is starting to give me a headache." Others will read it and say, "Wait a minute, Dave. You didn't explain the difference between the monthly average strategy and the monthly sum strategy. Well, I don't want to get too deep in the weeds of detail, dear reader. Some of these products have more than a few moving parts and, for the time I have to write this book, and the time you probably have to read it, I would rather give you a macroscopic bird's eye view than look at each of them with a microscope.

That having been said, however, if you see me or Drew personally, we will be happy to explain every nut and bolt of these products and fully explore their pros and cons until, as my grandmother used to say, "the cows come home." But I hope this has answered some of your questions about annuities. Whenever you do income planning for retirees, the subject always comes up in one way or another.

CHAPTER TWELVE

Getting a Round TUIT

"Do you know what happens when you give a procrastinator a good idea? Nothing!" ~ Donald Gardner

Some years ago I attended a seminar that featured a motivational speaker. I remember very little of what the man said, except for a point he made near the end about procrastination (he was not in favor of it).

The speaker left the podium and began walking up and down the aisles, handing each of us a wooden disc, about the size of a half-dollar, with the letters **TUIT** stamped on both sides.

"Has anyone here heard of Leo Greenwald?" He said as he distributed these wooden discs. None of us had.

"That's not surprising," he said. "Because Leo was a procrastinator." The speaker explained that Leo was his college roommate.

"Leo was very bright," said the speaker. "But he hated to study. He also loved coffee."

The speaker had our attention. We were all wondering what all of this had to do with anything.

Returning to the lectern, he said that when Leo knew a test was coming up, he would wait until the night before the day of the test and C.R.A.M., which he said stood for Create Rapidly Acquired Memory.

He said his roommate would often stay up well into the night, drinking coffee and studying at a local coffee house. The caffeine kept him awake. When the coffee shop closed around midnight, he would get four coffees to go, put lids on them and carry them back to the dormitory in one of those cardboard cup holders. He would drink coffee and continue studying into the wee hours.

The speaker explained that, back in the 1970s, coffee cup lids did not have pre-cut holes. The paper coffee cup people apparently assumed that you would transport the cup with the lid on, and then remove the lid and drink the coffee, just as you would from a ceramic cup. But Leo liked to take the lid off the cardboard cup, tear a crescent-shaped hole in the lid with his front teeth, put the lid back on the cup and sip from the hole. He said this served two purposes. It kept the coffee warmer longer and kept the coffee from splashing out

At this point, our curiosity was piqued big time. We were all wondering what this had to do with *anything*.

"Leo was very smart," the speaker continued. "He always passed his tests."

He said the next morning when he woke up he saw that Leo had fallen asleep at his desk. Beside him was a piece of paper on which Leo had doodled several sketches of coffee cup lids, each with holes of varying sizes and shapes drawn on them.

"Leo was inventing this," he said, holding up a white plastic coffee cup lid with a hole in it.

"Leo was bright, but he was also a procrastinator," said the speaker. "He was always going to apply for a patent for his coffee cup lid... one of these days... when he got ***around to it.***"

At that point, he held up one of the round wooden discs with TUIT on both sides and we all got the point. He asked us if any of us had anything we were going to do... one day... when we got *around to it.*

"Well, I have given each of you a **round TUIT**. So, now go out and **DO IT!**"

It was a pretty clever way to make a point, I thought.

As Paul Harvey used to say, and now... for the *rest* of the story:

The speaker went on to explain that Leo never got around to filing a patent on his coffee cup lid. And as it turned out, he was not the only one in the world with the idea. A patent for the lid with a hole in the top was eventually filed by Kenneth Dart, of the Dart Container Corporation, who made a fortune with it. All Leo got out of the deal was a good story to tell at dinner parties.

If you have come this far with me, dear reader, I hope you have gained something from this book you did not have before. I commend you on your thirst for knowledge. Have you come away with a broader understanding of wealth preservation? Do you have a better grasp of planning for retirement and the pitfalls that await those who fail to plan? Do you agree with me that it is usually a series of small decisions you make as you go through life that lead you to either success or failure? Is the pathway to a happier and more secure retirement clearer for you? If you answer in the affirmative, then I have accomplished part of my mission. My ultimate goal is to empower you as an investor and saver to take action on what you know.

The notion that knowledge is power is only partially right. Knowledge not acted upon is merely knowledge. Applied knowledge is power.

Knowledge is a collection of facts. Think of it this way: I know that I am standing on a railroad track. That is a fact. I see a train coming. Another fact. I know the train is made of hard steel and that my soft body would not survive a collision with the train.

Again, another fact. But I only **benefit** from this knowledge if I take action by stepping off the tracks and avoid the approaching train.

Since I began my career as a financial professional in 1995, I have heard many of the reasons people give for postponing taking action to secure their financial future. Here are a few of them:

I'm Too Busy

"I'm too busy," is the one I most often hear from young adults who are busy raising families and building careers. To them, retirement is way off on the far horizon. Something they will worry about later in life (when they get around to it). As a card-carrying baby boomer, I can tell you that time goes by very swiftly. That distant horizon will loom right in front of you all too soon. Every day you fail to plan is a day that is lost and gone forever. Take advantage of a free consultation with a qualified fiduciary financial professional and, if nothing else, just talk. It never hurts to explore your options.

It's Too Late to Plan

The earlier the better, true, but it is never too late to start making arrangements for your future. I keep my ear pretty close to the ground, and I am here to tell you there are new strategies and new products becoming available every day in the field of retirement planning. Even if you have already retired, you may be surprised at what may be available that would benefit you.

It's Too Soon to Plan

Some people have the idea that you shouldn't start planning for your retirement until you are five years away from it. Nothing could be further from the truth. I advise people to start saving as soon as they begin working and to start developing strategies by their mid-20s. It's never too soon, folks.

I Can Handle It Myself

Remember the health/wealth comparison in Chapter Ten? Just as you trust your health to a professional, do the same with your wealth. The idea of self-dentistry or self-surgery is laughable, isn't it? But losing thousands of dollars in your portfolio isn't so funny. Neither is paying thousands of dollars in unnecessary taxes. At least, have a conversation with a professional fiduciary and explore your options. You will never know if you are paying too much in taxes until you have an expert examine your returns.

I've Got Everything Covered

If you really do, that's wonderful. But are you sure? Are you sure the amount you are saving is enough? Are you sure you won't out-live your resources? Even if you have saved enough, do you have a distribution plan that will last for the next 30 years or so? Does your plan take taxes and inflation into consideration? Are you positive your money is invested in the right place to achieve all of your ob-jectives? It never hurts to get a second opinion.

Don't Know Where to Start

Admitting this is the first step. All the more reason to search for a financial advisor to help you sort things out and help you under-stand where you are now and where you want to go. Financial plan-ning can be intimidating without a guide. If you think your finances are in such a mess that you don't know where to begin, start at the beginning. Have a friendly conversation with an advisor you trust and get an objective viewpoint. It may not be as bad as you think.

So what's your reason? Let's hope you have already taken action to preserve your financial future. If not, Drew and I would welcome the opportunity to meet with you. If nothing else, we will consider it a privilege to become acquainted with you and hear your story.

Have you ever said to yourself, "If I only knew then what I know now?" At the beginning of this book, I told you about my parents, Clifford and Sue Blackston. They were loving and caring parents, and I loved them very much. When my father died relatively early at age 65 of a lung condition he contracted working for the railroad, I had no idea what financial planning was. I have often wondered what would have happened had I been able to go back in time and share with my parents what I later learned. If only I could have convinced them, when they were at the peak of their young lives, to at least talk to a financial professional, life would have turned out much differently for my mother, who struggled financially after Dad died. Could I have convinced them of the importance of paying more attention to that aspect of their lives? I don't know. My father was an intelligent man, but he was stubborn, too. My mother was wise in many areas of life, but, unfortunately, she spent more time planning the family dinner than she did our financial future.

Today's baby boomers who are staring retirement in the face like to quote the trendy mantra that 60 is the new 40. That may be true in the respect that we are, on average, living longer. But for the purposes of planning, 40 is still 40, and 60 is still 60. My advice? Don't wait until you get around to it to do it. Start taking control of your financial future now!

ABOUT DAVID BLACKSTON

David is a Registered Financial Consultant®, Certified Estate Planner®, Certified Senior Advisor®, Investment Advisor Representative, licensed insurance agent and member of Ed Slott's Elite IRA Advisor Group. He hosts a daily radio show on the "Rob Newton Resource Hour" and speaks at numerous educational workshops monthly. David has more than 40 years of experience in the financial industry.

He began his career in the banking industry in 1973, working up to senior vice president of a regional bank in central Kentucky. After realizing his passion was in serving the needs of individuals and families, David founded Blackston Financial Advisory Group, LLC. His steadfast dedication to client needs and financial expertise has built a financial firm that prides itself on client service and family-oriented values.

David's unique approach to financial planning includes investment advisory services, tax forecasting and estate planning — all working together to provide a comprehensive plan for clients. His methods include safe money and risk money, and how these two competing worlds can be brought together to provide a worry-free lifestyle. Blackston Financial Advisory Group is also a member of the Better Business Bureau.

David is active in his church and is an individual partner with different ministries around the globe. He is married to Andrea Blackston and has two children: Drew, also an advisor in the office, and Kyle, a professional golfer.

ABOUT DREW BLACKSTON

Drew is a Registered Financial Consultant® who has been work-ing in the financial services industry since graduating from the Uni-versity of South Florida in 2008 with a bachelor's degree in business administration. He began his career focusing on individual specific health needs before expanding into market research and financial planning. After spending two years on the investment policy com-mittee and involved in the day-to-day trading of client accounts, Drew decided to move into the individual financial planning field. His unique perspective during the financial crisis prepared him for the future not only with market research and analysis but with asset preservation.

He specializes in investment strategies, stock market analysis and asset preservation. A native of Elizabethtown, Kentucky, Drew is a national Investment Advisor Representative, Registered Finan-cial Consultant®, registered insurance agent and notary public for the state of Florida. He completed his Certificate for Financial Plan-ning through Kaplan University. Drew is married to Valerie

Blackston, who is director of communications with Blackston Financial Advisory Group.

ACKNOWLEDGEMENTS

There are so many people that I want to thank. First, our staff for all that they do for me, without them we could not be where we are today. Then I would like to thank Advisors Excel, and more importantly Shannon Kruger and his team for inviting me to become a part of this fantastic group. His help and the programs that Advisors Excel offered me have made me a much better advisor. I also want to thank Bill Kentling and Mallory McDaniel of the Advisors Excel Creative department for all of their advice on this book, along with Tom Bowen, our writing consultant, who was instrumental in helping Drew and me produce this book.

The team at Blackston Financial Advisory Group.

Made in the
USA
Lexington, KY